INCOTERMS® RULES *FOR AMERICANS®*

(Rewritten for Incoterms® 2020 Rules)

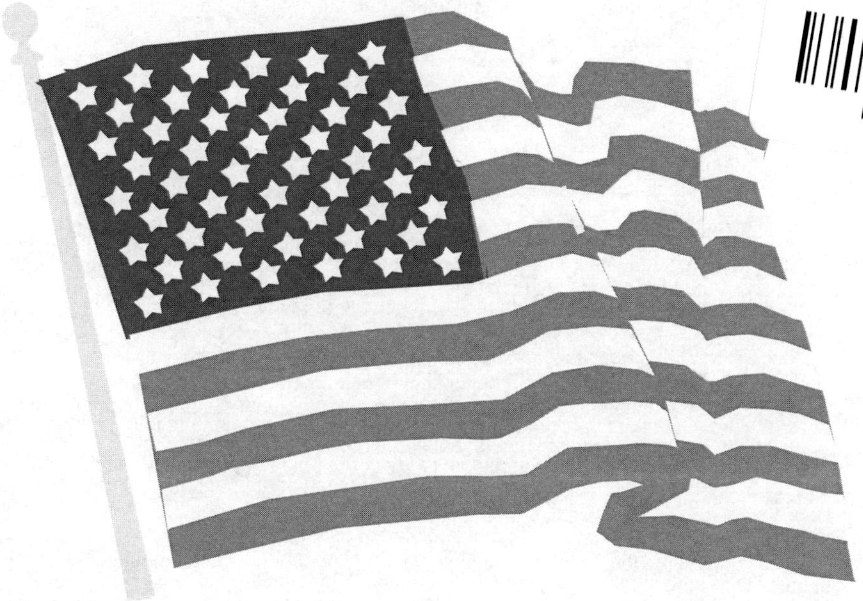

Simplifies and answers questions about Incoterms® 2020 rules from an American perspective.

by **Frank Reynolds**

This publication has not been produced or endorsed by the ICC. Instead, it is written to explain the role of these rules from a U.S. viewpoint for Americans and those desiring to do business with us.

TABLE OF CONTENTS

PREFACE & ACKNOWLEDGEMENTS		i
INSTRUCTIONS ON HOW TO USE THIS BOOK		iii
PART I – HISTORY		1
Chapter 1	Developments Outside Incoterms® [1] Rules	3
Chapter 2	Summary of Major Changes in Incoterms® 2020 Rules	5
PART II – BASIC CONCEPTS		7
Chapter 3	What Incoterms® 2020 Rules Are & Aren't, Do & Don't Do	9
Chapter 4	Role of Incoterms® 2020 Rules in Sales-Purchase Contracts	11
Chapter 5	Offers and Proforma Invoices	17
Chapter 6	Getting Goods from Seller to Buyer	25
Chapter 7	Transportation Terminology	29
Chapter 8	Insurance	33
PART III – COMMENTARY ON INDIVIDUAL INCOTERMS® 2020 RULES		37
Chapter 9	Introduction to Part III and Story Line	39
Chapter 10	Ex Works	41
Chapter 11	F-Group Rules	51
Chapter 12	Free Carrier	53
Chapter 13	Free Alongside Ship	73
Chapter 14	Free on Board	81
Chapter 15	C-Group Rules	87
Chapter 16	Carriage Paid To	89
Chapter 17	Carriage and Insurance Paid	97
Chapter 18	Cost and Freight	103
Chapter 19	Cost Insurance and Freight	109
Chapter 20	D-Group Rules	115
Chapter 21	Delivered At Place	117
Chapter 22	Delivered at Place Unloaded	123
Chapter 23	Delivered Duty Paid	131
Part IV – AMERICANA		137
Chapter 24	An American Perspective	139
Chapter 25	What Happened with the UCC Shipment and Delivery Terms	147
INDEX		151

[1] Incoterms® is a trademark of the International Chamber of Commerce, registered in several countries.

PREFACE & ACKNOWLEDGEMENTS

Our new title, *Incoterms® Rules for Americans®* is our fourth edition. It has been written to cover *Incoterms®*[2] *2020* rules. Old friends will note that this title differs slightly from previous versions. The inclusion of "rules" comes at the request of the International Chamber of Commerce (ICC), which prefers that "Incoterms®" be used as an adjective rather than a noun for trademark reasons. It has registered the word "Incoterms®" in the United States and other countries as its trademark, which accounts for the first of the registration symbols. The second trademark covers the title itself, which belongs to my company, International Projects, Inc.

There are several reasons for this fourth edition. The most obvious is that the International Chamber of Commerce produced *Incoterms® 2020* rules. The second is to explain what happened with the shipment and delivery rules that are once again found in §2.319 through §2.324 of the Uniform Commercial Code, and how their near deletion affected U.S. domestic business. Third, like its predecessor, sales of the 2010 *Incoterms® for Americans®* approached 10,000 copies which indicates that many people found it useful. It is also an important material in our seminar program. Finally, as I mentioned in previous versions, one learns a lot over ten years.

The composition of this Drafting Group differed from its predecessors. I was no longer the only non-European, but was joined by delegates from Australia, China, and Turkey. I was also not the only trader; two other delegates added their hands-on practical experience to the usual legal knowledge. The result was a more user-friendly and less Eurocentric set of rules and recommendations. For this I owe a huge thank you to the two co-chairs David Lowe (UK) and Christophe Martin Radke (France) as well as my other Drafting Group colleagues:
Ercument Erdem (Turkey)
Virginie Jan (China)
Burghard Piltz (Germany)
Bob Ronai (Australia)

We also received invaluable help from Special Advisor Charles Debattista. Besides being probably the world's foremost living authority on Incoterms® rules, Charles can express complicated issues in an easy to follow manner. Readers will see his handiwork in the introduction and explanatory notes found in the official *Incoterms® 2020* book.

For the second time the Drafting Group was moderated by another American, Emily O'Connor, who is the ICC's Director of Trade and Investment. As with the 2010 revision, Emily kept us on track, using tact and ready wit to productively channel our frequently argumentative discussions. She also put each successive draft together which entailed managing thousands of comments received from many of the ICC worldwide member organizations. In addition, we all received considerable help from the ICC's Florence Diao-Gueye, Policy Assistant, Knowledge Solutions.

The actual drafting process started with a questionnaire and request for comments sent to the approximately 130 ICC National Committees in as many countries. Based on the replies, the Drafting Group submitted the first proposed draft to the National Committees for comment. A second and third round of proposed drafts

[2] Incoterms® is a trademark of the International Chamber of Commerce, registered in several countries.

and National Committee comments followed, until approval was finally secured from the ICC's Commercial Law and Practice Commission in Paris on October 24, 2018.

Start to finish, the Drafting Group physically met three times in Paris, twice in London and once in Beijing. There were also numerous meetings of the co-chairs, email exchanges, conference calls, and even an outreach meeting with an expert in letters of credit.

There are two other people for me to thank besides my 2020 Drafting Group colleagues. Until his death in 2018, Professor Jan Ramberg was the world's foremost Incoterms® authority. He was also a very kind gentleman who graciously welcomed this rookie into the Drafting Group in 1998. Finally, but by no means least, my wife, Kitty Callahan, kept me focused as usual and provided critical editorial help. So, Kitty, as with the three previous versions, this one's for you.

Frank Reynolds
Toledo, Ohio, July 15, 2019

INSTRUCTIONS ON HOW TO USE THIS BOOK

This book is designed to be read cover-to-cover. Even readers already experienced in contract formation, such as lawyers, should do so. Reading about an already familiar topic will demonstrate the basic level at which this book is written, and enable you to better interpret topics with which you are less familiar. In order to facilitate this chore, most of the book is deliberately written in small easy-to-read chapters.

Parts I and II are akin to setting the table. Once done, the rules themselves in Part III proceed quickly and easily. We used some updated versions of the proforma invoices from the previous edition and added new ones to illustrate our expanded story lines. Our examples are just that, proforma invoices. If they were examples of actual commercial invoices for U.S. exports, the issue of a destination control statement would need to be addressed. When first reading the book cover-to-cover, you will find some repetition from one rule to another - for which I do not apologize. Once you have read it through, you will likely revisit one or several individual rules from time to time. When you do, it is important that you find everything you need where you expect to find it.

Please understand that this book is merely a commentary, designed for use with rather than instead of the official *Incoterms®*[3] *2020*[i] book. The official book is also designed to be read cover-to-cover as much can be gained by comparing the rules to each other. The expanded introduction to the new official book is particularly important. Readers will quickly appreciate Professor Debattista's ability to express even complex issues in an easy to follow manner. As mentioned in our preface, he is probably the foremost living expert on Incoterms® rules.

The official *Incoterms® 2020* book (ISBN 978-92-842-0510-3) is available in the U.S. from the United States Council for International Business at www.uscib.org/international-business-bookstore. It is required reading for anyone interested in Incoterms® rules.

So why bother reading this book? Incoterms® rules are written for general use in all countries. Some rules work better than others in the United States, which is where this book is particularly useful. Further, these rules come from a drafting group where lawyers predominated, and are written in a more-or-less lawyerly manner. Since I was part of this group, I can explain the rules in clear American business English. I have been exporting and importing for well over 50 years, and know how trade works in practice as opposed to mere theory. Finally, I have been instructing Incoterms® rules and their effect on related topics for over thirty years, and know which issues Americans find most difficult to grasp. Although this book provides these assets, the official rules are found only in the official *Incoterms® 2020* book.

Although Incoterms® rules are designed only for use in sales-purchase contracts, they influence disciplines beyond sales and purchasing. For instance, the credit departments of sellers using secured payment terms should be concerned with control of the documentary process. This relates to forwarder and carrier selection. Same goes for compliance people for items requiring enhanced export control. Import managers at buyers of containerized cargo may want to control transportation to ensure timely ISF[4] filings. Naturally, transportation people at both seller and buyer firms should be seeking comparative freight costs. Best practice is to make sure all concerned parties are aware of the new Incoterms® version.

---

[3] Incoterms® is a trademark of the International Chamber of Commerce, registered in several countries.

[4] Importer Security Filing

Do not try to use every Incoterms® 2020 rule. Only the very largest users will find all eleven useful. Most users focus on only four or five rules in the normal course of business. So why bother learning the others? The answer is that your counterparty may propose a rule with which you are not familiar, so it is best to know what is involved. It is also useful to see how each rule differs from all others. Once you have read the official rules and this book cover-to-cover, go back over the rules you believe will be most useful. While doing so, be sure to keep your role in mind as some rules favor sellers while others favor buyers. Readers who both buy and sell will need to refocus from one situation to another.

This book uses the expressions "pre-carriage," "main carriage" and "on carriage," which in American lingo mean inland freight on the seller's side, transport from seller's side to buyer's side, and inland freight on the buyer's side. See the Transportation Terminology chapter 7 for how these play out in carriage contracts.

We also use the terms "seller's side" and "buyer's side" with international transactions. This enables us to locate tasks that are typically done either in the seller's country (export clearance, pre-carriage) or in the buyer's country (import clearance, on-carriage, unloading). This makes perfect sense for Americans. We are not involved in a customs union, so shipments to and from all countries require both export and import clearance. This applies even to Canada and Mexico with which we have both free trade agreements and land borders. It makes less sense within customs unions which is one reason this distinction is not used in the official rules. It also makes less sense for domestic transactions, so for these think "before carriage" and "after carriage," at least for domestic door-to-door shipments.

The word "omnimodal" may appear strange. It is a real word, appearing in the ICC's *A to Z of International Trade*[ii] dictionary, and means all modes of transport. This is not to be confused with "multimodal" which means transport by more than one means.

Our presentation of the rules differs from the official *Incoterms® 2020* book. Beginning with the 2010 version, the omnimodal rules have been separated from the marine-only rules in the official ICC books. This was done to discourage the inappropriate use of marine-only rules in transactions for air, ground or containerized vessel shipments. It works well in practice, and the logic remains sound. However, your writer has learned through many seminars to American audiences that these rules are easier to grasp when they are presented in letter group order rather than divided by means of transport. Doing so enables us to consider the things that the rules within each group have in common. (For example, all D Group rules are used in arrival contracts.) In doing this, we will follow a modified and updated version of a chart found in the *Incoterms® 2000*[iii] version, along with likely accompanying places and appropriate transport modes.

GROUP E DEPARTURE:
EXW – the place where shipment originates (omnimodal)

GROUP F MAIN CARRIAGE UNPAID:
FCA – either the place from which the shipment originates or another agreed place on the seller's side (omnimodal)
FAS – alongside a vessel at a port on the seller's side (marine only)
FOB – loaded on a vessel at a port on the seller's side (marine only)

GROUP C MAIN CARRIAGE PAID
CPT- an agreed place on the buyer's side (omnimodal)
CIP – an agreed place on the buyer's side (omnimodal)
CFR – an agreed port on the buyer's side (marine only)
CIF – an agreed port on the buyer's side (marine only)

GROUP D ARRIVAL
DPU – an agreed place on the buyer's side (omnimodal)
DAP – an agreed place on the buyer's side (omnimodal)
DDP – an agreed place on the buyer's side (omnimodal)

Each letter group except EXW has a heading section which describes what the rules in that group have in common. Be sure to read them as well as the individual rules. (There is no letter group heading page for EXW as it is the only rule in the departure group.)

From time to time we will show task line references such as A2-B2. These refer to the matching columns in the official ICC book, with Column A listing seller tasks and Column B listing buyer tasks.

Finally, be careful with visual aids like wall charts that do not come from the ICC. Some well meaning service providers attempt to provide overdetailed coverage of rules on an 8 1/2 x 11 sheet of paper. This almost always leads to skipping important possible applications. One common error is limiting the place used with FCA to *either* the point where a shipment originates *or* the point where main carriage begins rather than permitting both possibilities. Another is limiting the place used with CPT and CIP to the point where main carriage ends, rather than *any* agreed place on the buyer's side. In both cases, the likely reason is that the designer ran out of room on a single sheet of paper! By contrast, the drawings accompanying each rule in the official ICC book and the official ICC wall chart are well thought out and reliable.

---

[i] *Incoterms® 2020*, ICC Publishing SA, Paris, France, ICC Publication no. 723E, ISBN 978-92-842-0510-3

[ii] *A to Z of International Trade*, Frank Reynolds, ICC Publishing SA, Paris, France, ICC Publication no. 623, ISBN 92 842 1277 4.

[iii] *Incoterms® 2000*, ICC Publishing SA, Paris, France, ICC Publication no. 560, ISBN 92-842-1199-9

PART I – HISTORY

CHAPTER 1 - DEVELOPMENTS OUTSIDE INCOTERMS® RULES

This is a non-exhaustive list of events in no particular order that have occurred since Incoterms®[1] 2010 were released. Some may affect the choice of Incoterm® for U.S. buyers and sellers. Some may require additional care in vetting trading partners. Others may lead to restructuring transaction models or trading relationships.

- Revision to the UCC withdrawn: The 2004 revision to the Uniform Commercial Code deleting the shipment and delivery terms found in §2-309 through §2-344 was rescinded in 2011 because of industry opposition.

- Verified Gross Mass regulations: Effective July 1, 2016, the U.N. International Maritime Organization SOLAS regulations require that marine carriers receive certified total weight of containers plus contents prior to vessel loading.

- U.S. Export Control Reform (ECR): Work continues toward merging much of the U. S. Munitions List (USML) and the Commerce Control List (CCL).

- U.S. Unified Bureau of Industry & Security and State Department destination control statement: In November 2016, a unified BIS /ITAR destination control statement was released. (15CFR 758.6). The destination control statement requirement is now limited to the commercial invoice. Shipments of exclusively EAR99 tangible items are exempted.

- U.S. Low Value import shipment duty exemption increased to $800 of imported merchandise per person in a single day.

- U.S. Export Control Reform Act of 2018 (ECRA): establishes legal authority for export controls beyond the Export Administration Act of 1979.

- U.S. Entity List and Unverified List (Export Administration Regulations part 744) expanded.

- U.S. enacts Countering American Adversaries Through Sanctions Act (CSAATSA)

- U.S. issues executive orders for sanctions on certain Venezuelan persons, entities and digital currency (the petro).

- U.S. issues executive orders imposing "Certain Sanctions in the Event of Foreign Interference in a United States Election."

- U.S. issues Global Magnitsky Sanctions Regulations (31 CFR part 583) implementing the Global Magnitsky Human Rights Accountability Act.

---

[1] Incoterms® is a trademark of the International Chamber of Commerce, registered in several countries.

- U.S. pulls out of the Trans-Pacific Partnership.

- U.S. pulls out of the Iran Nuclear Deal (Joint Comprehensive Plan of Action - JCPOA).

- European Union imposes Blocking Regulation (Council Regulation 2271/96) to mitigate the effect of U.S. Iranian sanctions.

- U.S. tariff policy – 232 and 301 punitive duties:
  Buyers: Increased duties on aluminum and steel from many countries and on many Chinese origin products may cause sourcing changes.
  Sellers: retaliatory duties on US origin products can dry up formerly attractive markets and increase pressure to develop new export markets.

- U.S. duty drawback regulations revised:
  US Customs and Border Protection published new final rules in December 18, 2018 edition of the Federal Register. Merchandise substitution standards liberalized, record keeping requirements simplified, timelines for filing claims extended and standardized.

- KOR-US Trade Pact renegotiated

- USMCA replaces NAFTA:
  The U.S.-Mexico-Canada Agreement provides many changes, including switching liability for documenting a claim from the exporter to the importer, elimination of a required form, broadening availability of advance rulings, expedited processing of express shipments, and many more. (Still awaiting ratifications as of July, 2019.)

- U.S. Foreign trade zone rules revised:
  Direct delivery expedited by means of e214.

- U.N. IMO low-sulfur bunkers requirement: increased freight costs, longer transit times, and possible capacity reduction for marine transport, effective January 1, 2020.

- BREXIT?

- Proposed new Routed Transaction rules from BIS and Census (not released as of July, 2019).

- New OFAC reporting rules (in comment period as of July, 2019).

CHAPTER 2 - SUMMARY OF MAJOR CHANGES IN INCOTERMS®[2] 2020 RULES

It is difficult to judge the impact of a revision to the Incoterms® rules so soon after it is completed. Still, a pattern has become obvious when comparing the last few revisions. It seems that major revisions alternate with lesser ones. 1990 saw a major rewrite, as for the first time seller – buyer tasks were aligned side by side in the now familiar A1 through 10 and B1 through 10 format. The 2000 version at first seemed limited to tidying up some loose ends. However, it turned out to be huge, as it made the previously cumbersome FCA rule far more user-friendly. As a result, this rule has become widely used. 2010 brought another major rewrite, reducing the total number of rules from 13 to 11. It was well received and deliberately written in non-legalese language. However, it continued the 1990 and 2000 exception to F-Group rules where sellers would handle main carriage, which I consider a flaw and ignore as a viable option. (See the F-Group Rules chapter for details.) 2020 first appears to be another limited revision in terms of number of changes. However, the entire matching column lineup has been revised, and there are several changes in substance that have the potential for significant improvement in the way business is done. Sadly, the F-Group flaw was carried forward. Time will tell how this revision compares to its predecessors.

Here are the more significant changes.

1. The introduction has been expanded. It had been shortened for 2010 as many users skipped over previous introductions. However, it became obvious that more was required. The result is a larger useful introduction written by Charles Debattista. Charles writes as though he were speaking to the reader, and the new introduction is an absolute joy to read.

2. The list of seller-buyer tasks A1-A10, B1-B10 has been revised according to relative importance in the sales-purchase contract:

A1-B1	General Obligations
A2-B2	Delivery
A3-B3	Transfer of Risks
A4-B4	Carriage
A5-B5	Insurance
A6-B6	Delivery / Transport Document
A7-B7	Export / Import Clearance
A8-B8	Checking / Packaging / Marking
A9-B9	Allocation of Costs
A10-B10	Notices

   Note that Delivery and Transfer of Risks have been moved up to the second and third positions, reflecting their importance.

3. The Guidance Notes found in the 2010 version have been expanded and renamed "Explanatory Notes." Lawyers assure me that this will make them more useful to arbitrators in dispute resolution. Illustrations have also improved.

4. Insurance was addressed in several ways. First, it now has its own task line in recognition of its relative importance. Second and more important, the seller's default obligation to insure under the

[2] Incoterms® is a trademark of the International Chamber of Commerce, registered in several countries.

CIP rule has been changed from so called "minimum cover" (Institute Cargo Clauses C or "free of particular average" in American) to "nearly maximum cover" (Institute Cargo Clauses A or "almost all risks" in American). However, the former Institute Cargo Clauses C has been retained as the default seller obligation in the CIF rule. See the Insurance chapter 8 for details.

5. DAT has been replaced by DPU. In the 2010 version, DAT was introduced to replace the former marine-only DEQ, broadening the reach to include any transport mode and any transport-related place, i.e. "terminal." Because it is the only rule explicitly tasking the seller with unloading, it became useful for situations like machinery installation where the accompanying place is other than a terminal. In order to accommodate such use, the rule was changed to Delivered at Place Unloaded (DPU). Of course, terminals are included in this broader range of places.

6. Provision is made for parties to use their own means of transport rather than contracting for it. For international transactions this will most likely effect pre-carriage and on-carriage. Truck fleets owned by sellers and buyers are common in domestic trade.

7. Costs are shown in greater detail both under A9 - B9 Allocation of costs and in the task heading to which they pertain (such as A7- B7 Export/ import clearance).

8. An attempt is made to reconcile the FCA rule with the requirement for on-board documentation frequently imposed by banks in their letters of credit.

9. As it is obvious to Americans purchasing the official *Incoterms® 2020* book or e-book, the price remains high. This is primarily in developed countries and was done to permit reduced pricing in developing countries, where paying \$60, \$70, or more per copy was a real hardship. This price discrimination seems unfair at first, but significantly broadening the access to these rules increases their value to all who use them. Given the increasing amount of trade with and within the developing world, their decision seems valid.

PART II – BASIC CONCEPTS

CHAPTER 3 - WHAT INCOTERMS® 2020 RULES ARE & AREN'T, DO & DON'T DO

The following short list describes the boundaries where Incoterms®[3] operate. They are described in detail throughout this book.

WHAT INCOTERMS® 2020 RULES ARE:

- 11 terms of shipment and delivery developed by the International Chamber of Commerce (ICC) for business-to-business sales-purchase of tangible portable goods.
- Country neutral, but for international use are influenced by the United Nations Convention for the International Sale of Goods (CISG).
- Available worldwide through the nearly 130 ICC national committees and affiliates.
- Updated to reflect current trade practice (average life span is 10 years).
- Drafted in English and widely translated.
- Legacy to a long tradition of international use since 1936.
- Increasingly used in domestic trade.
- Written to reflect rather than direct trade practice.
- Always abbreviated by a three-character English language acronym.
- Always accompanied by a geographic place – the more precise the better.
- Self-contained.

WHAT INCOTERMS® 2020 RULES AREN'T:

- Law. Incoterms® rules should be specified in contracts order to apply: acronym + place + version (Incoterms® 2020).
- All inclusive.

WHAT INCOTERMS® 2020 DO:

- Divide costs and risks between sellers and buyers.
- Guide parties to subsidiary contracts (such as carriage and insurance).
- Address compliance issues such as export and import clearance.
- Mirror responsibilities in 10 task matching column lists which serve as handy checklists.
- Above all, reduce the potential for seller-buyer misunderstanding.

WHAT INCOTERMS® 2020 RULES DO NOT DO:

- Form a complete contract in themselves.
- Address passage of ownership.
- Address revenue recognition. (However, accounting rules such as GAAP and IFRs do consider issues addressed by Incoterms® rules such as delivery and transfer of risk.)
- Address remedies for breach of contract.
- Address more than one transaction. (Drop shipments are usually combined transactions.)
- Automatically apply – particularly important with transactions covered by the law of a common law U.S. state where the presumption might be in favor of UCC shipment and delivery rules.
- Address U.S. tax avoidance devices (such as passing risk at the limit of U.S. territorial waters).
- Address specific payment terms.

[3] Incoterms® is a trademark of the International Chamber of Commerce, registered in several countries.

- Address unloading, except for DPU.
- Lend themselves to overdetailed charts. (The illustrations found in the official *Incoterms® 2010* book are not overdetailed and may be safely followed.)

CHAPTER 4 - ROLE OF INCOTERMS® RULES IN SALES-PURCHASE CONTRACTS

The following mantra headed this chapter in our 2010 edition: *Nothing is more basic to successful repeat business than a meeting of the minds between seller and buyer.* It is no less true today. Where do most commercial problems start? Misunderstanding - misunderstanding between sellers and buyers, between sellers and their own factories, between either party and carriers. For international transactions, add the potential for misunderstanding between exporters and their freight forwarders, importers and their customs brokers, banks and everyone else, and failure to observe applicable government regulations.

Throughout this book we are considering business-to-business sales and purchases of tangible, portable goods. For economy of words, we will refer to such transactions as "sales contracts," although buyers would likely call them "purchase contracts." Regardless of which you call them, they are contracts between sellers and buyers.

Before going further, I need to remind you that I am not a lawyer. Nothing in this book should be considered legal advice. Rather, it is the practical recommendations of an experienced international trader with an extensive background with Incoterms®[4] rules.

Incoterms® rules were developed for international trade where there is tremendous potential for uncertainty. By definition, goods pass from one country to another. In international trade this often involves different languages, different business norms, different cultures, different standards, different currencies with changing exchange rates, and two or more different bodies of law. Sellers and buyers are often located further apart than is true for domestic business, sometimes in very different time zones. Greater distance usually means higher transportation costs, making returns of incorrect goods very costly. Also, with transport by sea, weeks may pass after shipment before anyone becomes aware that a problem exists.

The potential for confusion is not limited to international transactions. For many years, we Americans have been using the shipment and delivery terms that are again found in §2-319 through §2-324 of the Uniform Commercial Code (UCC). These terms are not easy to understand, particularly as everyone's favorite - FOB - morphed into versions for use in both freight prepaid and freight collect situations and both shipment and arrival contracts. When using them, we often think we know what we are doing, and likely know what we want to happen, until controversy occurs which often brings surprises to one or both parties. This is probably a major reason these terms had been deleted from the UCC as obsolete in 2004 as part of a major revision to Part 2. However, this revision was itself repealed in 2011 for reasons having little to do with the shipment and delivery terms.[5] The result is that they remain in the contract law of all U.S. common law states[6].

Readers involved in both international and domestic business realize the inconvenience of using Incoterms® rules for international trade and the UCC terms domestically. Despite the fact that the UCC terms still exist, there is likely to be a continued shift towards the domestic use of Incoterms® rules for reasons of convenience rather than law as larger companies standardize around them for all transactions. This may well mirror the ripple effect that introduced e-commerce, when major companies insisted that their suppliers communicate with them electronically, causing the suppliers to require the same of their own vendors, and so on.

---

[4] Incoterms® is a trademark of the International Chamber of Commerce, registered in several countries.

[5] The now-repealed 2004 revision to the UCC consisted of 308 pages, of which only 4 pages covered the deletion of §2-319 through §2-324.

[6] All U.S. states except Louisiana

TERMS OF SHIPMENT AND DELIVERY IN SALES CONTRACTS

There are more contracts involved in business-to-business sales transactions than meet the eye. Someone must provide for non-product services to get the contract goods into the buyer's hands. We ship so often that we can lose sight of the fact that every shipment is actually a contract of carriage between someone (seller or buyer) and a carrier. One also hopes that someone is arranging for insurance to cover the goods in transit, and this is another contract.

Shipment and delivery terms such as Incoterms® rules answer the questions "who does what" and "who pays for what" by tasking the parties. This usually means one party or the other providing non-product services like transportation and insurance. Whoever does so is normally in a position of selecting and contracting with the service providers, and providing instructions as part of these contracts. The contracting party is therefore in a position to exert more control over the service provider than is the other party.

Carrier and forwarder selection are particularly important in international trade, where open account payment terms are less common than in domestic business. Some frequently used payment terms like commercial documentary letters of credit and documentary collections rely on correctly executed documentation to work properly. Some critically important documents are prepared by forwarders and carriers, so selection of these service providers is an important payment term consideration. It makes little sense for a seller to insist on a documentary credit without the ability to instruct these service providers about the preparation and disposition of the required documents. This would logically lead sellers relying on accurate documentation toward those Incoterms® rules that task them with providing main carriage transportation – as with the C-Group and D-Group.

In Incoterms® 2020 rules, as with previous versions, only two rules speak to insurance - CIP and CIF. All other rules are silent. Both CIP and CIF require the seller to provide insurance. However, a major change occurred for 2020. While CIF sellers may satisfy this obligation by providing minimum cover, the default coverage for CIP sellers is now Institute Cargo Clauses A (roughly equivalent to our incorrectly named "all Risks"). Please refer to the Insurance chapter 8 for details. This is not to say that no insurance is required for the other rules. Far from it. Practical considerations dictate that for the other rules the parties are best served by deciding who should insure elsewhere in the sales contract.

There are numerous government regulations that require compliance. All trade, even domestic, is regulated for hazardous materials and consumer product safety. International regulations are far more complex. All countries have some sort of import clearance regulations, and the U.S. has what are probably the most demanding export regulations of any free world nation. There are also country- specific product standards like the EU CE Mark and Mexican NOMS, and environmentally driven rules like the U.S. Lacey Act. Meanwhile, cargo security concerns have brought a seemingly endless series of regulations in the post 9/11 world. Once again, Incoterms® rules help answer the question "who does what," by assigning such tasks as export and import clearance and cargo security information to sellers and buyers.

SHIPMENT CONTRACTS VERSUS ARRIVAL CONTRACTS

Sellers and buyers need to agree at what point the seller's responsibility for the condition of the contract goods should end. For convenience, we divide sales contracts into two broad categories:

- Shipment contracts - where the seller's risk ends when the goods are made available or handed over to a carrier.
- Arrival contracts - where the seller's risk ends when the goods arrive at the agreed place.

Incoterms® rules address this under A2-B2 DELIVERY, which indicates the risk transfer point for all eleven rules. EXW is used in shipment contracts, as delivery takes place when the goods are made available to the buyer. F-Group and C-Group Rules are used in shipment contracts, as delivery takes place when the goods are handed over to a carrier on the seller's side of any main carriage. D-Group rules are used in arrival contracts, as delivery takes place only after the goods arrive at the agreed place on the buyer's side.

The difference between shipment and arrival contracts goes beyond risk transfer. Mandatory accounting rules such as GAAP and IFRS indicate when revenue on sales may be recognized. A common thread throughout these rules is that the seller's risk for the condition of the contract goods must have ended. The time difference between shipment and arrival can be significant – such as a shipment by vessel from the U.S. East Coast to Australia. See Revenue Recognition in the American Perspective chapter 24 for details.

OTHER SALES CONTRACT CONSIDERATIONS

Important as shipment and delivery terms are, they do not address all issues in a sales contract. It is important that sellers and buyers clearly agree on what they want to happen. Failure to do so can lead to disputes that in turn can result in arbitration or litigation. If contracts are silent about important issues, the governing law will likely impose its own "gap-fillers." This can have surprising results.

Since Americans and many other people enjoy pretty broad contractual freedom, it is best to specify whatever you believe important in your contract. The following checklist may be helpful.

- identities and addresses of seller and buyer
- description of items exchanged (goods and/or services) and pricing
- terms of shipment and delivery, preferably using an Incoterms® rule
- place of shipment and/or delivery and/or arrival
- terms of payment
- passage of ownership
- timeline for performance
- applicable law
- dispute resolution method and procedures
- names and capacities of signatories.

Failure to specify these in the contract can lead to some strange "gap-filler" results. Here are a few samples from the UCC: If a contract is silent about when payment is due, the default position is that it will be at the point where the buyer is to receive the goods (UCC §2-310). If the place is not specified, the default position is that it will be at the seller's place of business (UCC §2-308). If the manner of delivery is not specified, the default position is that it will be a single shipment (UCC §2-307). If title passage is not specified, it will be when the seller "delivers" (UCC §2-401).

It well may be that neither seller nor buyer had anything like these in mind when entering into the agreement. One of the nice things about Incoterms® rules is that using them practically forces the parties to consider most of these important issues.

WHAT INCOTERMS® RULES BRING TO SALES CONTRACTS

As well defined shipment and delivery terms, Incoterms® rules bring certain benefits to business-to- business contracts for the sale/purchase of tangible, portable goods.

- They come from the private sector International Chamber of Commerce (ICC) rather than law. This means that they reflect trade practice rather than attempting to legislate it. It also means that they can be revised to reflect changes in trade practice, and since 1980 this has been done about every ten years.

- They have been used in international trade since 1936 and are widely understood worldwide. They are also translated into many languages.
- A growing number of US companies are considering Incoterms® rules for domestic use.
- Incoterms® rules are self-contained. All you really need is right between the covers of *Incoterms®2020*[7], particularly as the introduction has been expanded.
- All Incoterms® rules have three-letter English language abbreviations.
- All Incoterms® rules must be accompanied by a geographic place, forcing the parties to consider what they are doing.
- Every Incoterm® rule is divided into 10 tasks in matching columns for quick reference. (Column A lists the seller's tasks and Column B lists the buyer's.) Besides providing handy checklists, this system guides the parties into additional contracts, such as transportation, that may be needed to complete the transaction. It also alerts the parties to possible regulatory compliance issues.
- Above all, Incoterms® rules reduce the potential for seller-buyer misunderstanding. This is the reason they exist.

CAVEATS

Besides noting the benefits Incoterms® rules bring to contracts, users should be mindful of their limitations.

- As mentioned earlier, Incoterms® rules are not law and do not automatically apply unless specified in the sales contract. The preferred way of doing this is to write the abbreviation of the rule you are using and the accompanying place, followed by "Incoterms® 2020."
- Incoterms® rules do not indicate where ownership passes from the seller to the buyer. This important point should be addressed elsewhere in the sales contract.
- They do not address breach of contract issues. However, B3 and B9 of all Incoterms® 2020 rules provide for premature passage of risk and cost if the buyer fails to fulfill certain obligations.
- They are not all inclusive. Sellers and buyers must determine particular issues for themselves, such as how a given port or airport handles cargo in and out, what regulations a particular country imposes, etc.
- They do not remove the need of the parties to specify an accompanying place, hopefully in as much detail as possible.
- "Drop shipments" can cause problems when the parties do not think things through. For instance, Party A (seller) sells goods to party B (buyer). Goods are manufactured by Party C, who may even be in a third country. The goods are to proceed directly from Party C to Party B. Which Incoterms® rule applies? The answer is that there are really <u>two</u> contracts involved. Party A is the seller in its sales contract with Party B, but is the buyer in its purchase contract with Party C. Depending on the relationship between Party A and Party C, these two contracts may or may not use the same Incoterms® rule. There's also the very practical concern that the correct documents should go to the correct party, which can require close monitoring.
- Stretching the FOB term: Americans accustomed to using the Uniform Commercial Code shipment and delivery terms may be tempted to use the UCC FOB term for freight prepaid arrival contracts internationally and for all modes of transportation. This causes confusion as (with the unfortunate exception shown in the following bullet) main carriage is not tasked to the seller in any of the F-

---

[7] *Incoterms® 2020*, ICC Publishing SA, Paris, France, ICC Publication no. 723E, ISBN 978-92-842-0510-3

Group Incoterms® rules. Further, the FOB Incoterms® rule is limited to use with waterborne main carriage. More in the FOB Chapter.

- Exception to main carriage obligation in FAS, FOB and FCA: If the seller and buyer agree, this exception requires the seller to contract for main carriage at the buyer's risk and cost. I suggest this not be done except for special circumstances. The C-Group Incoterms® rules adequately address situations where the parties want the seller to contract for main carriage at the buyer's risk and cost without resorting to this exception. Merely arranging for main carriage without contracting for it is another thing entirely, and this should obviously be done at the buyer's risk and expense.
- Carriage obligation in FCA when accompanied by a location other than the seller's premises, FAS and FOB: A4 of FAS, FOB and FCA states that the seller has no obligation to the buyer to contract for carriage. This means main carriage. In order to deliver, the seller must provide pre-carriage to get the goods to the place specified:
  with FCA when other than the seller's premises,
  next to the vessel for FAS,
  and on the vessel for FOB.
- The US Government does not officially recognize Incoterms® rules, although they are mentioned in some regulations.
- For US exports, there is an apparent conflict about export reporting between the Census Bureau's Foreign Trade Regulations and the F-Group Incoterms® rules. There is a way around this which we will address in the Introduction to F-Group Rules chapter 11 and the American Perspective chapter 24.
- The reportable value for U.S. exports often differs from the actual selling price. The correct value formula is indicated for each rule in its respective chapter.
- The use of D-Group Incoterms® rules may delay revenue recognition under GAAP and IFRs accounting rules.
- D-Group rules do not normally work well with documentary letters of credit.
- Incoterms®2020 cannot address cargo security issues in detail. The differences in country specific regulations are simply too great, and the frequency at which these change would make any detailed coverage quickly obsolete. Security regulations are specifically tasked in Carriage A4-B4 and in Export/Import clearance A7-B7.
- The weighing obligations under the Verified Gross Mass regulation (U.N SOLAS Regulation 2) are not addressed in Incoterms® 2020.
- The phrase "if customary" is used throughout Incoterms® 2020 but is nowhere defined.
- Variants to Incoterms® rules are possible. However, to the extent that the parties depart from the standard division of tasks they should explicitly state their intentions in their contracts. To minimize the use of variants, parties should check to see if another Incoterms® rule better matches their intentions.
- As with the 2020 version Incoterms® 2020 are written in a modern gender-neutral style. This reduces the possibility of using pronouns, and the reader may require a while to become familiar with this.

CHAPTER 5 - OFFERS AND PROFORMA INVOICES

Our last chapter described the role of shipment and delivery terms in purchase/sales contracts, which we'll continue calling "sales contracts." Depending on the nature of the goods and the size of the deal, these contracts can be anywhere from volumes of tightly written text to a simple exchange of promises. We'll leave the massive contracts to lawyers, and use the often-quoted 80-20 rule which states that 20 percent of a company's customer base accounts for 80 percent of its business. This strongly implies numerous repeat sales, and these are frequently handled in a less formal manner.

Sometimes, frequent repeat sales are covered in a "master" (also called "frame") contract citing the general terms and conditions. Details that are more subject to change as time goes on are left to exchanges between sellers and buyers on a shipment-by-shipment basis.

Reminder, I am not a lawyer. What you read is based on a considerable amount of commercial experience rather than legal training, and is not to be construed as legal advice.

Bilateral contracts involve an exchange of promises. Someone makes an offer to another party. If that party agrees, it communicates its acceptance. Offers can be initiated by either party. Sellers can take the initiative by making offers to sell, commonly referred to as quotations. When buyers agree, they normally respond with purchase orders. Buyers can initiate the process by issuing offers to purchase, sometimes as unsolicited purchase orders. Sellers can indicate their agreement by issuing acknowledgments, or in some cases by actually shipping.

Regardless of who starts the process, sales contracts result whenever offers and acceptances are in substantial agreement. There are entire bodies of law written about what "substantial agreement" means, and many companies employ self-serving boilerplate language on the forms they use. We aren't going there. There are also bodies of law about how offers are deemed to be delivered, how they can be withdrawn, etc., and we aren't going there either. Suffice to say that offers and corresponding acceptances do the job the vast majority of times.

As you will see in the next chapter, there are more issues to address in international trade than is true of domestic business. For this reason, international trade is more structured and is more document intensive. After all, we are dealing with different countries with their particular regulations and often different languages. Savvy international sellers use documents called proforma invoices for their quotations. Since much of the information they contain should also be present in well conceived domestic quotations, readers primarily involved in domestic business should also find them interesting. Please also keep the minimum contract issues from the Role of Incoterms® in Sales Contracts chapter 4 in mind, as successful proforma invoices often become the seller's half of a sales contract.

PROFORMA INVOICES

These documents are often defined as "make believe invoices" and "sales quotations dressed up as invoices." Both are true. Proforma invoices are sales quotations in invoice form. They are used primarily in international trade because:

- They recite all the details the seller thinks are important for the transaction.

- Regardless of language or custom, just about everyone in business recognizes an invoice format for what it is.
- Governments understand them, and this can be particularly important when buyers require import licenses or foreign exchange allocation.
- When sales contracts result, proformas become models for the commercial invoices which follow.
- Parties using letter of credit payment terms benefit, as proformas provide "roadmaps" for banks to use in issuing credits.
- When constructed to itemize cost increments, they enable buyers to determine whether they or the sellers are better positioned to handle such tasks as freight and insurance. This would otherwise be difficult.
- They enable sellers to take the initiative by proposing the more seller-friendly Incoterms® rules (such as the C-Group).
- They make it easier for buyers to buy. Informed buyers want to know their total costs, not simply merchandise prices.
- A correctly prepared proforma invoice indicates a level of experience on the seller's part. This can be very reassuring to buyers, particularly in new business relationships.

Important as these reasons are, the biggest benefit proforma invoices bring is that they force sellers to think their transactions through. This usually means consulting with other disciplines. Sales must provide the merchandise pricing and its validity period. Credit must indicate acceptable payment terms. Those "highly imaginative" people in charge of product availability must opine as to when the contract goods would really be ready to ship in the event of an order. Speaking of time lines, buyers usually like to know when they can expect to receive the goods, particularly when sellers handle transportation. Obviously, both parties also need to determine which should handle transportation. This usually means sellers getting service availability and cost estimates from carriers and forwarders to offer buyers. Is insurance available, at what cost, and which party should procure it?

Each proforma invoice should indicate the following information:

- the date the proforma invoice is prepared
- a unique proforma invoice number
- a reference to the buyer's inquiry, if any
- the seller's name and address
- the buyer's name and address
- any intermediate consignees, if known
- payment terms
- term of shipment and delivery (Incoterm® rule + place + Incoterms®[8] 2020)
- a validity date to avoid an open ended commitment (often a number of days from the proforma invoice date)
- an estimated shipment date (often a number of days from the day an acceptable order is received)
- the currency of the transaction
- the body of law under which the offer is made and to apply to any resulting contract
- the point where ownership passes from seller to buyer
- the quantity of the goods offered
- product description of the goods offered (perhaps including the six-digit HS number)

[8] Incoterms® is a trademark of the International Chamber of Commerce, registered in several countries.

- unit price and total per line item
- total of all line items
- additional charges to conform to the cited Incoterms® rule. (Depending on the selected rule, these should include packaging and may also include where applicable: container loading, pre-carriage, forwarding, export clearance, heavy lift, origin terminal handling, main carriage, conveyance unloading, destination terminal handling, import clearance, on-carriage and insurance. We will cover these in the following chapter and again as we cover each Incoterms® rule individually.)
- a country of origin statement, if appropriate and important to the transaction
- any particular verbiage the customer's country may require if appropriate and if known.

The following proforma invoices are illustrative of the four groupings of Incoterms® rules: EXW, the F- Group, the C-Group and the D-Group. They reflect the same product and price information, and show the progression from EXW through the D-Group.

- Under EXW, the seller bears no transportation responsibility at all and delivers when the goods are available for pickup.
- Under FCA + place where shipment originates (usually the seller's premises), sellers are not responsible for pre-carriage. Under FCA + other agreed place on the seller's side, FAS and FOB, sellers arrange and pay for pre-carriage. (We will continue to ignore the ill-conceived freight prepaid F-Group exception.)
- C-Group and D-Group sellers arrange and pay for pre-carriage and main carriage. Depending on the agreed place, sellers may also handle on-carriage with CPT, CIP, DPU, DAP and DDP. Under CFR and CIF the destination is a port, so buyers arrange and pay for any on-carriage. (Keep in mind that with C-Group rules we are referring <u>only</u> to contracting and paying for transportation. Delivery happens when the goods are handed over to a carrier, <u>not</u> when they arrive at the agreed place.)

We chose CIP as one of our illustrations as it speaks to insurance. Note our description of coverage as "Institute Clauses A" which is the new default seller's minimum obligation. We also chose DAP along with the buyer's premises as it places most transport responsibility on the seller. Although the DAP seller is responsible for the condition of the goods until they arrive, there is no insurance obligation. Savvy sellers do insure, though, and many either bury the premium cost in their merchandise price or charge the buyer for it as a separate line item. We chose the latter in our example as some countries assess duty only on the value of the goods themselves. Note that the CIP and DAP proforma totals are the same as they include identical cost increments. Only the points of delivery differ (handed over to the carrier with CIP, buyer's premises with DAP) which the proformas do not illustrate.

Done correctly, proforma invoices show the buyer what the seller is prepared to do and at what price. By itemizing the cost increments, the strengths and weaknesses in delivered pricing can be pinpointed. When done consistently, they provide a database which makes subsequent proformas easier to prepare. Above all, they help avoid misunderstandings, thus making sellers and buyers more comfortable in dealing with each other.

Our proformas place items like governing law and dispute resolution right on the front as there is no back shown. In practice, these are often recited on the back of the document along with other boilerplate language.

PROFORMA INVOICE

EXPORTER International Projects, Inc. 1150 South McCord Road Holland, OH 43528 USA	**PROFORMA INVOICE #** EXAMPLE 1 **PROFORMA INVOICE DATE** September 20, 2020 **PROFORMA VALIDITY DATE** October 20, 2020 **EST'D SHIPMENT DATE** September 30, 2020
SOLD TO Callahan & Riddle Ltd. Maple Grove Plains London E2E Q94 ENGLAND	**TERMS OF PAYMENT** Net 30 days **SHIPMENT/DELIVERY TERMS** EXW 1150 South McCord Road, Holland, OH 43528 USA, Incoterms 2020
SHIP TO Pick Up	**TITLE** Ownership transfers when payment is received by seller

QUANTITY	UNITS	DESCRIPTION OF MERCHANDISE	UNIT PRICE	TOTAL
300	Each	How to Better Your Golf Game – HS 950490	5.00	1500.00

LAW & DISPUTE RESOLUTION: The U.N. Convention on Contracts for the International Sale of Goods (1980) shall apply to this offer and any resulting contract. Any disputes will be resolved by binding arbitration services of the International Chamber of Commerce.	**MERCHANDISE TOTAL** Export Packing	**US$** 1500.00 75.00
	GRAND TOTAL EXW Holland, Ohio	**US$** 1575.00

PROFORMA INVOICE

EXPORTER International Projects, Inc. 1150 South McCord Road Holland, OH 43528 USA	**PROFORMA INVOICE #** EXAMPLE 2 **PROFORMA INVOICE DATE** September 21, 2020 **PROFORMA VALIDITY DATE** October 21, 2020 **EST'D SHIPMENT DATE** September 30, 2020
SOLD TO Callahan & Riddle Ltd. Maple Grove Plains London E2E Q94 ENGLAND	**TERMS OF PAYMENT** Net 30 days **SHIPMENT/DELIVERY TERMS** FCA Air America Terminal 2, Columbus Airport, Columbus, OH, USA, Incoterms 2020
SHIP TO Air America Terminal 2 Columbus Airport Columbus, Ohio, USA	**TITLE** Ownership transfers when payment is received by seller

QUANTITY	UNITS	DESCRIPTION OF MERCHANDISE	UNIT PRICE	TOTAL
300	Each	How to Better Your Golf Game – HS 950490	5.00	1500.00

LAW & DISPUTE RESOLUTION: The U.N. Convention on Contracts for the International Sale of Goods (1980) shall apply to this offer and any resulting contract. Any disputes will be resolved by binding arbitration services of the International Chamber of Commerce.	**MERCHANDISE TOTAL** Export Packing Pre carriage	**US$** 1500.00 75.00 30.00
	GRAND TOTAL FCA Columbus Airport	**US$** 1605.00

PROFORMA INVOICE

EXPORTER International Projects, Inc. 1150 South McCord Road Holland, OH 43528 USA	**PROFORMA INVOICE #** EXAMPLE 3 **PROFORMA INVOICE DATE** September 22, 2020 **PROFORMA VALIDITY DATE** October 22, 2020 **EST'D SHIPMENT DATE** September 30, 2020
SOLD TO Callahan & Riddle Ltd. Maple Grove Plains London E2E Q94 ENGLAND	**TERMS OF PAYMENT** Net 30 days **SHIPMENT/DELIVERY TERMS** CIP Maple Grove Plains, London, England, Incoterms 2020
SHIP TO Same as SOLD TO	**TITLE** Ownership transfers when payment is received by seller

QUANTITY	UNITS	DESCRIPTION OF MERCHANDISE	UNIT PRICE	TOTAL
300	Each	How to Better Your Golf Game – HS 950490	5.00	1500.00

LAW & DISPUTE RESOLUTION: The U.N. Convention on Contracts for the International Sale of Goods (1980) shall apply to this offer and any resulting contract. Any disputes will be resolved by binding arbitration services of the International Chamber of Commerce.	**MERCHANDISE TOTAL** Export Packing Pre carriage Main carriage and on carriage Insurance (Clauses A)	**US$** 1500.00 75.00 30.00 190.00 23.07
	GRAND TOTAL CIP Maple Grove Plains	**US$** 1818.07

PROFORMA INVOICE

EXPORTER International Projects, Inc. 1150 South McCord Road Holland, OH 43528 USA	**PROFORMA INVOICE #** EXAMPLE 4	**PROFORMA INVOICE DATE** September 23, 2020
	PROFORMA VALIDITY DATE October 23, 2020	**EST'D SHIPMENT DATE** September 30, 2020
SOLD TO Callahan & Riddle Ltd. Maple Grove Plains London E2E Q94 ENGLAND	**TERMS OF PAYMENT** Net 30 days	
	SHIPMENT/DELIVERY TERMS DAP Maple Grove Plains, London, England, Incoterms 2020	
SHIP TO Same as SOLD TO	**TITLE** Ownership transfers when payment is received by seller	

QUANTITY	UNITS	DESCRIPTION OF MERCHANDISE	UNIT PRICE	TOTAL
300	Each	How to Better Your Golf Game – HS 950490	5.00	1500.00

LAW & DISPUTE RESOLUTION: The U.N. Convention on Contracts for the International Sale of Goods (1980) shall apply to this offer and any resulting contract. Any disputes will be resolved by binding arbitration services of the International Chamber of Commerce.	**MERCHANDISE TOTAL** Export Packing Pre carriage Main carriage and On carriage Insurance (Clauses A)	**US$** 1500.00 75.00 30.00 190.00 23.07
	GRAND TOTAL DAP Maple Grove Plains	**US$** 1818.07

CHAPTER 6 - GETTING GOODS FROM SELLER TO BUYER

In former editions this chapter was titled "Hoops and Hurdles." Readers kindly informed me that this cutesy name was absolutely useless when trying to locate the covered topics, so a name change was in order. By whatever name, it is a summary of things that must happen for a shipment to get from the seller to the buyer.

Whenever I do a live seminar on Incoterms®[9] rules, I proclaim one side of the room to be the seller's country and the other the buyer's. I then begin to walk across the room, starting from the "seller's premises" (which is represented by the wall on the "seller's side") and going toward the buyer's, ending with the "buyer's premises" (represented by the opposite wall). As I move along, I stop at the departure point from the seller's side, about ¼ of the way. This represents a seaport or an airport, and the walk to it simulates pre-carriage. I then simulate main carriage by proceeding to a point about ¾ of the way. This brings me to the arrival point on the buyer's side. I then finish walking to the far wall to simulate on-carriage to the buyer's premises.

My stroll is usually rewarded by a "now I get it" look from many attendees. All the tasks I describe along the way exist at least to some extent in all international shipments and to a lesser extent in domestic transactions. So, as good sportscasters say when broadcasting a football game on the radio: "moving from left to right on your dial."

INTERNATIONAL SHIPMENTS

At the place where shipment begins (usually the seller's premises)

- Someone must provide the goods. This is the seller. There's more, though. The goods should be the correct goods and they should be provided when promised. (Make sure those "highly imaginative" people in charge of product availability read this – many companies have at least one.)
- Someone must suitably package the goods. A8 of each Incoterms®2020 rule specifies that this must be appropriate for transport. I have another caveat about "appropriate for transport." If the seller is not involved in main carriage (as with EXW and FCA), and would not otherwise know how it is to take place, the buyer should provide any required packing information before the contract is concluded. Different transport modes require different degrees of packing, the most heroic being for non-containerized shipments by vessel. Buyers should agree to pay for reasonable packaging costs as receiving undamaged shipments is very much in their interest.
- Someone must load the collecting conveyance, and for all rules except EXW this is a seller obligation.
- Someone must arrange and pay for pre-carriage. This could be either the seller or the buyer, depending on the rule selected, its accompanying place, and how the contract of carriage is contracted (door-to-door, door-to-port or airport, port or airport-to-port or airport, port or airport-to-door).

At the departure point on the seller's side (a port, airport or possibly a border location)

- Someone should arrange for the goods to be received by the main carrier, and this would usually be the party handling main carriage transportation. For FCA + other location, the seller is not

[9] Incoterms® is a trademark of the International Chamber of Commerce, registered in several countries.

responsible for unloading the delivering vehicle, as the buyer-appointed carrier or forwarder would probably have the people and equipment to do so.

- Someone must arrange for and pay for main carriage. This may be either the buyer (EXW or F-Group Rules) or the seller (C-Group and D-Group Rules).[10]
- Before the shipment can leave the seller's country, someone must arrange and pay for export clearance. The U.S. does not impose export duty but some countries do, so importers beware. All Incoterms® rules except EXW make the seller responsible for export clearance, as it seems most logical to have people deal with their own governments whenever possible. However, for U.S. exports, the Census Bureau Foreign Trade Regulations dictate that if the forwarder is appointed by the buyer, as is usually the case with EXW and F-Group rules, the forwarder should report the export. There is a remedy for this which we will explain in the introduction to the F-Group rules chapter 11.
  Besides mere reporting U.S. exports, a determination must be made about whether a license is required and, if not, why not. For some items, the licensing process can be time consuming and with no guarantee of success. Savvy sellers of such items do their homework before executing a sales contract. Further, there are "bad guy" lists which over the years have been growing both in number and length. Trade with such people, companies and countries is prohibited or severely restricted.
  With the exception of EXW, B7 of each Incoterms® 2020 rule requires that the buyer assist the seller with information and/or documents if requested at the seller's risk and cost. Under EXW, the reverse is true under A7.
- Someone must load the main carrier. Main carriers who follow shipping schedules normally load their own ships and planes. Since they call on the same ports/airports, they have arrangements in place for this. However, non-scheduled carriers such as "tramp vessels" have no such fixed rotation, and may not be able or willing to load. The FOB Incoterms® rule accommodates this for waterborne shipments by holding the seller responsible for loading despite the fact that the contract of main carriage is between the buyer and the carrier. This makes it useful for vessel chartering, but inappropriate for containerized shipments with ship lines that load their own vessels.

At the arrival point on the buyer's side

- Someone must unload the carrier. The DPU rule specifies that sellers are responsible for unloading, so there is no doubt. For the other rules, unloading brings a potentially contentious issue, particularly for vessel transport. There is no set worldwide policy among carriers about who pays unloading and related terminal handling charges. Many contracts of carriage do not include unloading and other "destination charges" while some do. It may depend on the destination, in which currency the carrier wants payment, and local regulations. It may also depend on the bargaining power of the party negotiating transportation with the carrier, and who knows what else. Incoterms®2020 addresses this in the CPT, CIP, CFR, CIF, DAP and DDP rules by cautioning that sellers that incur unloading costs in their contracts of carriage are not entitled to recover them separately from buyers unless otherwise agreed.
- Someone must arrange import clearance. The logic of having people deal with their own countries continues here. All rules except DDP task the buyer with import clearance. With the exception of DDP, A7 of each Incoterms® 2020 rule requires that the seller assist the buyer with information and/or documents if requested at the buyer's risk and cost. Under DDP, the seller is responsible for import clearance and all import taxes related to import clearance. (VAT is no longer specified by name, but is surely included in "taxes.") B7 of DDP requires that the buyer assist the seller with information and/or documents if requested at the seller's cost and risk.
- Someone must arrange for on-carriage. Again, this could be the seller or the buyer, depending on the agreed Incoterms® rule, the designated place, and how the carriage contract is structured.

At the buyer's premises

- Someone must unload the delivering vehicle. The only rule that tasks the seller with unloading is DPU. Again, the default follows logic as the buyer would probably be better positioned to unload at

[10] We will ignore the ill-conceived freight-prepaid F-Group rule.

its own premises than would the remote seller. The parties can always agree otherwise in their sales contract if they really want to.

- While Incoterms® rules do not address this issue, common sense dictates that someone at the buyer's premises examine the condition of the incoming goods and claim on carriers and/or insurers as necessary. This nicely segues into the next topic.

How about insurance?

This should obviously be addressed while the sales contract is being negotiated. Only two Incoterms® 2020 rules, CIP and CIF obligate anyone to insure. Please refer to the Insurance chapter 8 and the CIP and CIF chapters 17 and 19 for details.

For the other Incoterms® rules, the parties need to consider their own risk positions in the transaction and agree on insurance coverage outside of the rule. For EXW and FCA + origin point, the seller bears no transport risk. For FCA + another place on the seller's side and FAS, the seller is at risk for pre-carriage. FOB has the seller at pre-carriage risk plus the risk to the goods during vessel loading. (Note: Many insurers offer "FAS/FOB coverage for this.) In CPT, the buyer bears the risk from the "first carrier" and should consider "warehouse to warehouse" coverage. Under CFR, the seller remains at risk through vessel loading. D-Group rules are used in arrival contracts where the seller remains responsible for the condition of the goods up to the agreed place. Savvy sellers insure accordingly.

There may be more involved than merely risk for the condition of the goods, which passes at "delivery" per A2-B2 of all Incoterms® rules. Regardless of where loss or damage occur, a buyer who prepays may want some assurance other than the possibility of hauling the seller into court. There are also such issues as security interests, retentions of title, liens, etc. which may well address post-delivery events. Insurance products exist to cover these, but we're getting beyond the scope of this book.

DOMESTIC SHIPMENTS

These start the same way international shipments do, with the seller providing the correct goods, appropriately packaged and loaded on the collecting vehicle. Fortunately, there are fewer tasks involved for most domestic shipments. A single carrier frequently provides door-to-door service. However, for large shipping pieces and commodities, there may be transshipments involving several different carriers in different modes with individual contracts of carriage. Think of moving a heavy turbine by rail, barge and finally by truck. Even air freight shipments may be handled on an airport-to-airport basis, picked up and delivered at either end by local carriers independent of the airline, or by sellers and buyers themselves.

There is no export or import clearance for purely domestic transactions. However, sellers should make sure they are involved in purely domestic transactions. For instance, if you receive an order from a US company, and that company will export the goods, you have a domestic transaction as far as export reporting is concerned. (You should still watch out for "red flags" that would indicate an unauthorized export, and it's always a good idea to insist on knowing the destination country for many reasons.) On the other hand, if you receive an order from a foreign buyer, with instructions to deliver to a forwarder here, you would be the USPPI with the forwarder filing the EEI. We will cover this further in the American Perspective chapter.

In-transit damage can happen to domestic shipments, and someone should insure them. Often, these are covered by inland-marine provisions of blanket policies.

CONTRACTS

Now that we've seen what needs to occur, let's look at the contracts that make them happen.

Forwarding contracts
Usually the party contracting for main carriage also engages a freight forwarder. Nowadays, the roles of forwarder and carrier have blurred as they are often affiliated. In any case, U.S. forwarders should require powers of attorney from parties engaging them.

Contracts of carriage
Carriage contracts are evidenced by transport documents. Refer to the Transportation Terminology chapter 7 for details.
Sellers using F-Group Incoterms® rules should make sure they have a right to the transport document if this is important to them. This is particularly important for payment terms such as documentary letters of credit and documentary collections. Don't forget, under these terms the contract of main carriage is between the carrier and the buyer, not the seller. Also, the forwarder is most likely working for the buyer.

Insurance contracts
Insurance can be purchased in several ways and from several parties (insurers, forwarders and carriers). Refer to the Insurance chapter 8 for details.

Customs brokerage contracts
Customs brokers represent importers to their national customs services. Requirements to become a licensed customs broker vary from country to country. In the U.S. they are demanding and require significant knowledge of Customs regulations and procedure. The use of customs brokers is optional here but some countries require that importers engage them.
U.S. regulations require that brokers obtain powers of attorney from their clients. Pending new regulations require brokers to acquire significant additional client information.

Payment Contracts
Sales contracts sometimes stipulate that payment will be made by letter of credit (L/C). There are two basic types, standby and documentary.

- A standby credit pays when something doesn't happen, for instance, when a payment it guarantees wasn't made or a contract it guarantees wasn't completed. Since it is impossible to prove a negative, these normally require mere certifications by the beneficiary that the covered event did not take place and that payment is due. Standby credits are used in both international and domestic trade
- A commercial documentary credit pays when something happens, and in the case of sales contract that "something" is normally a shipment. Events can be proven by documents, and as their name implies documentary credits will require the presentation of documents to trigger payments. Banks strictly apply the terms and conditions of a letter of credit, along with the governing letter of credit rules (*UCP 600* as of this writing) and a broader set of procedures called *International Standard Banking Practice* (ISBP). When sellers are L/C beneficiaries, it is important that they check the documentary requirements against the sales contract to make sure they agree. Obviously, they should also make sure they are capable of providing the required documents within any timelines.

CHAPTER 7 - TRANSPORTATION TERMINOLOGY

Transportation has its own vernacular. This chapter will describe the basics to determine how Incoterms® rules speak to transportation.

Incoterms®[11] 2020 rules refer to transportation as "carriage" and we will do so as well. Although not always obvious, all carriage is covered by a contract between someone and one or more carriers. With the possible exception of EXW, the seller or buyer (or an agent of one or the other) is tasked with this.
We Americans tend to use the term "shipper" loosely to mean the party providing the goods for transport. Normally, this is the seller. Strictly speaking, the seller is the shipper only when it contracts for carriage. Sellers who ship freight collect and therefore do not contract for carriage are really "consignors" rather than shippers. (Since in these situations the buyer contracts for carriage, the buyer is really the shipper.)

In a carriage contract, the party contracting with the carrier for carriage will be termed "shipper." While other terms such as "documentary shipper" exist, we will stick with this premise. The party contracting with the carrier is in a position to give instructions to the carrier with the expectation that they will be followed except for unusual and unforeseen situations. This provides the shipper with control of the goods while in transit and also of the resulting transport documentation which can be used to implement secured payment terms.

TRANSPORTATION LEGS

Although not mentioned in the Incoterms® 2020 rules, there are actually three types of physical carriage in most international transactions. This is not always obvious, as frequently a single carrier will handle more than one. For international transport, we will need to differentiate between the seller's side and the buyer's side. These indicate the respective sides of main carriage transportation and usually indicate places in the parties' respective countries but this is not necessarily the case. (For instance, an American seller might sell goods out of Canada to a French buyer for delivery in India, in which case Canada will be the "seller's side" and India would be the "buyer's side.")

- Pre-carriage: transportation from the place where the shipment originates to the point of departure on the seller's side (for example, inland freight from Toledo to the Port of Baltimore).
- Main Carriage: transportation from the seller's side to the buyer's side (for example, vessel shipment from Baltimore to Hamburg).
- On-carriage: transportation from the arrival place on the buyer's side to the ultimate destination (for example, from the Port of Hamburg to Berlin).

These carriage terms can be matched to seller-buyer carriage responsibilities in Incoterms®2020 rules.

EXW: no seller responsibility for carriage or even loading.
FCA: either

A) if the accompanying place is the place where shipment originates the seller must load the collecting vehicle but has no responsibility for carriage

[11] Incoterms® is a trademark of the International Chamber of Commerce, registered in several countries.

or

B) seller must load and is responsible for pre-carriage to the agreed place on the seller's side.

FAS: seller is responsible for pre-carriage to the agreed place alongside the buyer-appointed vessel.

FOB: seller is responsible for pre-carriage and loading on to the buyer-appointed vessel.

CPT & CIP: seller is responsible for contracting for pre-carriage and main carriage to the agreed place on the buyer's side, and possibly on-carriage if the agreed place is other than the arrival place.

CFR & CIF: seller is responsible for pre-carriage, vessel loading, and for contracting main carriage to the agreed port on the buyer's side.

DAP, DPU, DDP: seller is responsible for pre-carriage, main carriage, and any on-carriage to the agreed place on the buyer's side.

Note: With the C-Group rules the seller contracts (i.e. arranges and pays) for main carriage, but is not responsible for the condition of the goods during main carriage. With the D-Group rules, the seller is responsible not only for contracting for main carriage but for the condition of the goods until they arrive.

CARRIAGE CONTRACTS

The above transportation legs also enable us to list the following typical conditions found in carriage contracts.

- Door-to-door: a single contract of carriage including pre-carriage, main carriage and on-carriage.
- Door-to-port (or airport): A single contract of carriage including for pre-carriage and main carriage. Any on-carriage is done by others.
- Port-to-port or airport-to-airport: A contract of carriage for main carriage only. Any pre-carriage and on-carriage are done by others.
- Port (or airport)-to-door: A single contract of carriage for main and on-carriage. Any pre-carriage is done by others.

"Through carriage" is transportation including two or more transport legs, such as door to door, door to airport, etc. This can be an important consideration with the CPT and CIP rules as we will see in detail in their individual chapters where through carriage is used to include at a minimum pre-carriage and main carriage.

Liner terms

Several versions ago, the Incoterms® drafters decided to avoid using the expression "liner terms" as it is vague. For the purposes of this book we will use it with a stipulated meaning: carrier loads and unloads the vessel. (This is limited to vessels, but in practice air freight shipments are normally carrier loaded and unloaded as well.) The carrier doesn't have to physically load or unload but usually arranges for this to be done for it by stevedore companies or terminal operators. This typically is the case with container shipments, where full containers are delivered at a container yard for subsequent terminal handling and vessel loading. The reverse takes place at the arrival port. Costs for this may or may not be included in the total freight cost, and could be for the account of either the seller or the buyer, depending on the contract of carriage. The important point is that the carriers undertake to have this done so that sellers and buyers are not concerned about actually doing it.

Non-liner terms

Large breakbulk and commodity shipments are often made using vessels that are rented in whole or in part. This is called chartering and can be done by either the seller or the buyer.

There are numerous possible charter situations, and some types of product (grain, timber) have their own industry-specific standardized arrangements. We will deal only with the basics here as this will illustrate the use of the marine-only Incoterms® rules. We will also not consider stowing and trimming which, although often additional cost elements, take place after loading.

Sometimes, such contracts of carriage (called "charterparties") are written on liner terms where the carrier loads and unloads. However, frequently loading and/or unloading are handled separately. In this case, the word "free" means that the carrier is not responsible.
Free in and out (FIO) - loading and unloading not included
Free in, liner out (FILO) - loading not included but unloading is
Liner in, free out (LIFO) - loading is included but unloading is not.

Charterparties normally specify timelines (called laytime) when vessels will be available for loading. Coordinating delivery timing of cargo arrival with loading is important. There are usually freight cost penalties for delay (called demurrage) and possibly freight cost reductions for loading sooner than anticipated (called dispatch money.)

The points where the seller delivers with the four marine-only Incoterms® rules speak to the loading possibilities:
FAS – next to the vessel at the departure port
FOB, CFR and CIF: loaded on the vessel at the departure port.

The only Incoterms® rule that speaks to unloading is DPU. It tasks the seller with unloading. As it is an omnimodal rule, the place can be any agreed place on the buyer's side, such as a container de-consolidator, a truck terminal, an airport or even a place unrelated to transportation. It could also be used with a vessel under liner terms or one of the non-liner terms shown above (such as FILO).

Transport documentation
Documents play an important role in the world of transportation. They evidence that a contract of carriage exists between someone and a carrier. They indicate the terms of carriage (sometimes through a reference document that often goes unread). They indicate the party responsible for freight payment (prepaid or collect). To at least some extent they contain a description of the articles shipped. They also indicate where and when the carrier received the goods, their destination, and to whom the goods should be released on arrival. Carriers typically note any obvious damage at the point where they receive the goods, which is particularly important with shipments that are handed over from one carrier to another. For vessel shipments, the transport document can be structured to convey possession rights.

CHAPTER 8 - INSURANCE

Incoterms®[12] 2020 rules have devoted a separate task line for insurance to highlight its importance.

Insurance is probably the least understood topic in international trade. There are some obvious reasons for this. First, most things work as planned. Most shipments arrive where they are supposed to, free of loss or damage. This provides a sense of security so that adequate insurance cover is too often taken for granted – at least until something bad happens. Next, insurance has its own vernacular. "All risk" doesn't cover all risks, "free of" usually means not covered, "average" means loss, a voyage is sometimes called an "adventure," and "sue and labor" usually has nothing to do with legal action. Also, keep in mind that a "fortuitous event" can be either good or bad.

Lately, insurers tend to customize policies for large clients, so generalized statements about how insurance works become both difficult and risky. If this weren't enough, your writer is not an insurance expert and comes equipped with only many years of trading experience and common sense. The sole purpose of this chapter is to explain the change to the way insurance is handled in the Incoterms® 2020 rules along with some obvious implications. For anything else, consult a real insurance expert.

Once you have read this chapter, check your insurance coverage. If you have your own marine cargo policy, determine how coverage is applied to your transactions. If you purchase coverage on a shipment by shipment basis from a third party such as a carrier or forwarder, what perils are covered and for how long does coverage remain in force?

There are two basic kinds of casualty insurance used for shipments; marine cargo and inland marine. These can overlap and are sometimes blended in a single policy.

MARINE CARGO INSURANCE

This is the kind of coverage you would use for a shipment by vessel or air. It can also apply to ground transportation as included in "warehouse to warehouse" coverage. Normally each shipment is somehow reported to the insurer and premiums are based on use. (Again, this could differ with individually crafted policies.)

Marine cargo coverage can be transferred (usually from seller to buyer) by showing the transferee's name as the assured. Insurance certificates can also be written in negotiable form.

The only two Incoterms® 2020 rules that speak to insurance at all task the seller with providing it. Such coverage must be written so that the buyer or any other party with insurable interest can claim directly from the insurer. This is often usually by means of an insurance certificate or policy.

Readers should be aware that there are different sets of marine insurance clauses. The two Incoterms® rules that specify insurance, CIP and CIF, refer to Institute Cargo Clauses (LMA/IUA) which are English and are in wide general use. Fortunately, CIP and CIF also allow for any similar clauses. The clauses commonly used in the U.S. (American Institute of Marine Underwriters – AIMU) differ slightly from the LMA/IUA Institute Cargo Clauses.

---

[12] Incoterms® is a trademark of the International Chamber of Commerce, registered in several countries.

Terminology also differs from country to country. The beloved American "all risks" should really be called "almost all risks" and is typically issued with some exclusions such as "free of strike, riot, civil commotion, and war." Coverage for these perils is usually available, and should be obtained to approach true all-risk protection. "Warehouse to warehouse" coverage is the insurance equivalent of door-to-door, and is also a worthwhile enhancement. The closest LMA/IUA matchup to our "all risks" is Institute Clauses A. Like all risks, Clauses A coverage should be also enhanced by strike, riot, civil commotion and war. The opposite of all risk, i.e. minimum cover, is what we Americans call "free of particular average" (abbreviated FPA) which covers a bare minimum number of perils. (Note the use of "average" to mean loss.) The closest LMA/IUA matchup to this is Institute Clauses C.

Shippers of goods by vessel are exposed to another peril, general average (GA). This is a worldwide marine loss mitigation agreement under which ship owners and cargo owners proportionately reimburse those who were put at loss because of efforts preventing the total loss of a vessel, its crew, and its cargo. While seldom invoked, GA can be both expensive and complicated. Fortunately, most marine cargo insurance including FPA and Institute Clauses C cover the general average peril.

In former versions of Incoterms® rules the default for both CIF and CIP was Institute Clauses C. The possibility of the parties agreeing to additional coverage was mentioned, and the seller was required to obtain at the buyer's request and expense additional coverage if procurable. This remains the default position for CIF. However, the default position for CIP in Incoterms® 2020 is that the seller is to provide Institute Clauses A. This is a major change. It comes from the realization that most of the shipments made under the omnimodal CIP are manufactured goods requiring more extensive coverage than Clauses C provide. By contrast, many shipments made under the marine-only CIF are commodities which are more likely to be adequately covered by Clauses C. This change addresses reality. Even under past Incoterms® versions, experienced parties involved with shipments of manufactured goods would (or should) have specified more than minimum coverage. Also, it is amazing how inexpensive adequate insurance really is, often a fraction of one percent. (This is how we know that most things work!)

This change of default coverage could have an unintended consequence if the marine-only Incoterms® CIF rule is used inappropriately, such as for containerized vessel shipments. Unless the parties agree otherwise, the C Clauses would apply by default, and the coverage would likely be inadequate.

The other insurance responsibilities shown in the 2010 version remain unchanged in 2020: the amount should be 110% of the CIF or CIP value, in the currency of the contract, and cover from at least the point of delivery to at least the named destination.

Insurance is not a one-way street. The insurer is obligated to cover certain unfortunate situations, but is entitled to cooperation to help it recover some of the loss it pays out. The claiming party should promptly report loss or damage. It should also promptly claim on the carrier so this claim can be subrogated to the insurer. It should also protect the goods from further damage (called "sue and labor") with the expectation that the insurer will reimburse normal out-of-pocket costs. It may also be required to allow a surveyor (a "damage detective") to inspect the goods to determine the extent and probable cause of the damage.

Let's take a typical full container vessel shipment as an example. Absent obvious damage to the container itself, the first party to identify a problem would likely be the buyer. Job one is to claim on the delivering carrier. Granted, it may not be the culprit, but this will trigger a series of claims along the supply chain protecting the insurer's subrogation interest. The insurer must also be promptly notified as it may wish to send a surveyor. The goods should be protected from further damage, perhaps by separating damaged from undamaged, storing in a covered area, or other means appropriate to the nature of the goods. Most insurers provide reimbursement for normal out-of-pocket sue and labor costs. To process the claim, the insurer will require documentation such as the commercial invoice, shipping document(s), carrier claim documents, packing list, possibly a survey report and evidence of insurance. Photographs of the damage and the packing are also helpful.

One defense that insurers can use is inadequate packaging. A8 of each Incoterms® rule requires sellers to provide packaging appropriate for transport[13]. Where appropriate, savvy sellers routinely photograph their packaged shipments, showing shipping marks for ready identification.

Both CIP and CIF require the seller to provide premium-paid evidence of insurance enabling the buyer to claim directly from the insurer. This puts the claiming burden on the buyer. Savvy sellers go a step further by providing buyers with the insurers' contact information which could be as simple as a website address.

How about the D-Group rules where the seller remains responsible for the condition of the contract goods through arrival at the agreed place? While there is no Incoterms obligation to insure, prudent sellers do so in their own interests. As shown earlier, claiming usually requires a level of cooperation from the buyers. Savvy sellers build this into their sales contracts when using D-Group rules.

Unless otherwise agreed, F-Group sellers protect their interests by insuring at least to the delivery point, which will normally be somewhere on the seller's side.[14] FAS and FOB sellers with inland marine policies should check whether coverage extends to shipside or vessel loading. If not, FAS-FOB coverage is usually available to cover any gap.

INLAND MARINE INSURANCE

This is the kind of insurance that is designed for domestic use. It is usually written to cover all domestic shipments for a single predetermined premium. Individual shipments are not reported. At the end of the policy term period, the insured informs the insurer the total number of shipments and their average value. The insurer then sets a new single premium for the next period based on this information and the loss record.

The increasing use of Incoterms® rules with domestic transactions presents a minor conflict. Both the CIP and CIF rules specify that the buyer must be able to claim directly from the insurer. However, with inland marine coverage, claims are usually made by the policy holder (i.e. seller) rather than by the buyer. This can be bridged by the parties agreeing that the seller will claim on its insurer on the buyer's behalf.

CARRIER PROVIDED INSURANCE

Some carriers offer insurance on shipments they transport. This may be expressed as an insurance premium or an additional value charge increasing the carrier's liability. Either should show up on the transport document.

This would be difficult to use with the CIP or CIF Incoterms® rules, as both require that insurance be placed so that the buyer or anyone else with insurable interest can collect directly from the insurer. As a further consideration, would you rather be claiming from an independent insurer or from the party that may have caused the loss or damage in the first place?

FORWARDER PROVIDED INSURANCE

---

[13] EXW sellers are not involved in any transport. FCA sellers may not be aware of the transport methods as this rule is omnimodal. If less than obvious, buyers should inform sellers of any extraordinary export packaging required (such as for transport by vessel as opposed to air). Savvy sellers ask when in doubt to avoid problems and to demonstrate concern for their customers.

[14] Again, the unfortunate F-Group main carriage paid exception creates uncertainty as sellers contract for main carriage at buyer risk and cost.

Most forwarders with their own master cargo policies resell coverage to their shipper-clients who do not have their own policies. This is usually coverage from an actual insurance company rather than the carrier-provided insurance mentioned above. As this coverage is resold by the forwarders, it is normally costs more than if placed under a shipper-owned policy. However, as previously mentioned, insurance is relatively inexpensive. Also, such coverage is relatively standardized and may not be appropriate for some situations or cargo types. Finally, few forwarders are truly insurance experts, and their experience is often limited to the off-the-shelf coverage their standardized policy provides.

A FINAL WORD

As the Incoterms® rules have changed, and as insurance is very complicated to mere mortals outside the industry, readers should consider devoting some time to it. A good place to start is the American Institute of Marine Underwriters' website. Enter AIMU all risk in your browser to get there. You will find the complete *All Risk*, *With Average*[15] and *Free of Particular Average* clauses, all revised in 2004. There are even cheat sheets comparing AIMU clauses with Institute clauses. However, none of this replaces consulting a true insurance expert.

---

15 "With Average" is coverage falling in between maximum (all risk) and minimum (free of particular average). It is not referenced in CIP or CIF.

PART III – COMMENTARY ON INDIVIDUAL INCOTERMS® 2020 RULES

CHAPTER 9 - INTRODUCTION TO PART III - STORY LINE

Now that we've done our preliminary work, it's time to cover the eleven Incoterms®[16] 2020 rules themselves. This introduction will explain our approach and provide some orientation.

Part III will summarize the parties' responsibilities, with particular emphasis on American use. I will also call your attention to points I think may appear odd at first, and explain them in everyday business English. Payment term implications for international transactions will also be mentioned.

It is often easier to narrate than to simply present bare facts. This worked well in the past, so we'll continue following a story line. Those of you have kindly read previous versions of *Incoterms® for Americans®*[17] will recognize some characters we've used to demonstrate how Incoterms® rules are used in (almost) real life situations. These characters have done their jobs well for over 25 years and it would be a shame to kill off old friends just for the sake of a rewrite. However, this time there are some new examples – remember what I said in the introduction about learning a lot over ten years. Increasing the number of usual suspects would only diminish the their usefulness in examples, so we will just add a few walk-on characters doing cameo roles and will briefly explain who they are as they turn up. For now, just skim read the remainder of this introduction as each character will be re-introduced as they appear in various scenarios.

Otto is a third generation German buyer. Like his father and grandfather before him, he is a widget importer, speaks no English, and has never visited the United States. Their warehouse is located in Baden Baden, an inland German location. The company has been doing so well that the entire older generation has retired and moved to Tahiti, leaving poor Otto to run the company on a "learn by doing" basis.

Glotz Industries manufactures widgets at Fort Wayne, Indiana, an inland U.S. location. Years ago, its sales manager located Otto's grandfather as a potential customer. An excellent relationship developed, and Otto's company became one of Glotz's largest accounts. The sales manager retired, and all shipping records were lost in a flood. No one there speaks German, or knows anything about Baden Baden other than "that's where we had been shipping all those widgets."

The idea of Otto and Glotz being able to do business with each other over the language barrier seems like a recipe for disaster. However, they can communicate at least basic contract related information by using *Incoterms® 2020* which is available in both English and German. They both understand and recognize proforma invoices and purchase orders. They have also purchased a basic sales contract abstract from the ICC, and use that as a template for structuring their translations. Above all, they trust each other, thanks to the long standing relationship the two companies enjoy.

Andre is a French widget manufacturer located in Strassburg, about 30 minutes by train from Baden Baden. He had been supplying Otto for years, but lost a substantial amount of business to Glotz. The fact that Germany and France both use the Euro alternatively helps and hurts, depending on the U.S. dollar exchange rate.

Gordon Lefevre (Gordie) is a Canadian widget importing distributor located in North Bay, Ontario. He began importing Glotz's widgets soon after they became duty free under the NAFTA. As he buys on net-30 day payment terms, there's no concern about documents except for the NAFTA origin certificate which Glotz provides once a year on a blanket basis. Presumably, they will need only switch forms for the USMCSA.

Mexican battery manufacturer Gerardo Jesus Prieto de la Torre (Jerry) uses Glotz's widgets as a component at his Monterrey factory. Like Gordie, he buys on open account payment terms, requires a NAFTA certificate

---

[16] Incoterms® is a trademark of the International Chamber of Commerce, registered in several countries.

[17] Incoterms® for Americans® is a registered trademark of International Projects, Inc., and Incoterms® is used by International Projects, Inc. with International Chamber of Commerce permission.

of origin, and will switch procedures for USMCA. Since the import clearance process is more demanding than in Canada, Jerry uses a freight forwarder-customs broker with offices in Laredo, Texas and Nuevo Laredo, Mexico.

Riddle Enterprises is a Seattle-based domestic distributor which has been handling Glotz's widgets for many years. Business is done on open account payment terms. Riddle normally places large orders for freight savings, but sometimes needs next-day delivery to supply an urgent customer requirement.

The following is a brief list our new walk-ons. They will be re-introduced as they turn up in their various scenarios. Jamal Bey has a small widget importing company in Casablanca, Morocco. Resinas de Oscar is a hapless French resin importer/speculator. Nihon Machinery Brokerage is a Japanese used machinery dealer. The Cutting Edge Manufacturing Company builds widget manufacturing machines. The Furna Hotel & Resort is a resort hotel at Cabo Verde. Zap Electrics is a British manufacturer of diesel electric generators. Venezuela Fuerza was a Venezuelan power company back in more prosperous 1970s and has nothing to do with present political conditions. Thai Pride uses the generous $800 US de-minimis threshold for small shipments to U.S. retailers under the DDP rule. One new player, J. W. Wescott Company, deserves special mention. It has been providing vessel to vessel lighterage in the Great Lakes for well over 100 years, and has America's only floating zip code (48222).

We'll assume that you already have a copy of the official *Incoterms® 2020*[18] book, and suggest that you keep it handy. Its Illustrations can help to bring concepts home. Comparison with familiar situations and documents is another means of illustration. Proforma invoice suit this purpose admirably, and we will see them as part of our story line for each Incoterm® rule.

[18] *Incoterms® 2020*, ICC Publishing SA, Paris, France, ICC Publication no. 723E, ISBN 978-92-842-0510-3

CHAPTER 10 - EX WORKS

Abbreviation: EXW
Transport mode: all (or more precisely, none)
Contract type: shipment
Place: where the shipment begins (usually the seller's premises)

Ex Works (EXW) is the Incoterms®[19] rule with minimum seller responsibility. All the seller needs to do is have the goods suitably packaged at the stipulated place and at the agreed time, and promptly notify the buyer that they are ready. The seller merely supplies the goods without any transportation arrangements, so it falls to the buyer to arrange them. Further, the seller is not responsible for loading the collecting conveyance, and delivers once the goods have been made available. Finally, under EXW **and only under EXW**, the seller has no export clearance obligation. (See the American Viewpoint section of this chapter for the reason this doesn't work well for us.)

Since the seller undertakes no transportation responsibility, the stipulated place is usually the seller's own premises or another location under the seller's control. This should be described in geographic terms in as much detail as possible, including addresses, such as EXW 1150 South McCord Rd., Holland, Ohio, USA, Incoterms® 2020.

EXW may be used with all means of transport. For this reason, the seller's obligation to suitably package may largely depend upon the buyer making the seller aware of the transportation arrangements, particularly for export orders. For instance, if the buyer gives the seller reason to believe that shipment will be made by air, and changes plans without the seller's knowledge, the seller would not know to provide the more robust packaging required for ocean shipments.

At first, EXW seems attractive, particularly for sellers who are concerned about getting involved with shipping and export control. All the seller need do is have the product ready to ship when agreed, put it in a suitable box, get it to the loading dock, and notify the buyer. However, a quick visit to the American Viewpoint section of this chapter will reveal the downsides.

EXW is so one-sided that buyers have difficulty with it. In fact, it really took some imagination to come up with suitable export scenarios. One possibility would be for sales of goods that are not destined for export or transport in the immediate future, such as goods in a foreign trade zone. There is also a common use in purely domestic transactions with small package carriers whose drivers typically load their trucks.

BUYER-SELLER RESPONSIBILITIES

The following is a short list of responsibilities.

1. **Goods and Payment**
   The seller must have the goods available when promised, suitably packaged, and must notify the buyer that they are available for pickup. The buyer must pay the seller.
2. **Loading the collecting conveyance**
   The seller has no responsibility to load. Common practice is that the seller does load, and most would willingly exceed their responsibility under this rule. However, this can open the door for controversy in case of damage during loading. This term does work for shipments with carriers that typically load their own conveyances such as with small packages.

---

[19] Incoterms® is a trademark of the International Chamber of Commerce, registered in several countries.

3. **Pre-carriage**
   The seller is not responsible. This presents no particular problem with domestic shipments. No particular problem for international shipments if buyers have "door-to-somewhere" carriage contracts or a forwarding agent in the seller's country. When this isn't the case, buyers could be put in an awkward situation of trying to arrange pre-carriage in foreign countries.
4. **Export clearance**
   This is a buyer responsibility under this rule. Regardless, U.S. export regulations bring the seller into the picture as the United States Principal Party in Interest (USPPI). See the American Viewpoint section of this chapter. U.S. importers could also face problems complying with the export control regulations of their suppliers' countries. Also, some countries charge export duty.
5. **Other hoops and hurdles**
   The seller is responsible for compliance with any transport security regulations through delivery, which in this case takes place before shipment begins. It must provide the buyer with any information on transport security regulations that it has in its possession. Since security regulations change often and vary from country to country and from one transport mode to another, Incoterms® rules are limited to making the parties aware that they must be addressed. This is covered in A4-B4 and A7-B7.
6. **Insurance**
   Neither party is required to insure under EXW. However, common sense dictates otherwise, and insurance should be addressed outside of the rule. This is particularly important for buyers because the seller delivers prior to loading or any transportation.
7. **Documentary implications**
   a. Commercial Documents: The seller should provide a commercial invoice, a packing list, and any other commercial documents cited in the sales contract.
   b. Transport Documents: The seller is not required to provide a transport document as the buyer is contracting for all transportation. In fact, under B6, the buyer must provide the seller with proof of having taken delivery.
      An exception could be a freight collect pre-carriage bill of lading where the seller exceeds its obligation by loading the collecting conveyance, or with a carrier that handles loading.
   c. Export Control Documentation: The seller has no obligation to the buyer for export clearance. However, as the USPPI the seller is obligated to provide company and product specific information to the buyer-appointed agent for EEI filing.
   d. Import Entry Documentation: This is a buyer obligation. However, A7 requires the seller to provide assistance at the buyer's request, risk and cost.
8. **Payment terms considerations**
   By definition, the buyer must arrange for pick-up at the stipulated place under the EXW Incoterms® rule. It then follows that the seller must be prepared to turn the goods over at that place. Since there's no way to use documents to restrict possession of the goods, the credit decision becomes either total trust (open account) or no trust at all (advance payment).

STORY LINE

Otto and Andre

Otto is a young importer of widgets located in Baden Baden, Germany. Andre is Otto's French widget supplier, located in Strasbourg, France, quite near the German border. Otto sometimes buys from Andre using the EXW Incoterms® rule as shown in Andre's proforma invoice EXW 1. He simply drives his truck to Andre's premises, loads, and returns home to Baden Baden, usually in time for lunch. Pre-carriage, main carriage and on-carriage are all handled by Otto in his truck. There is no export clearance or import clearance formalities between France and Germany as both are EU members.

Otto and Glotz
Otto wishes to purchase from Glotz Industries, a Fort Wayne widget manufacturer. Although the parties have enjoyed a longstanding relationship, neither has access to the way business had been conducted in the past. Both are literally starting from scratch.

As shown in proforma invoice EXW 2, Glotz's proposed the EXW Incoterms® rule in their first price quotation to Otto. The idea of making transportation arrangements from a factory in an unknown part of a foreign country - in compliance with unknown export control and cargo security procedures - was more than Otto was prepared to handle. He requested Glotz to assume more of the transaction burden by quoting under a different Incoterms® rule. We'll see the results in subsequent chapters.

Gordie and Glotz
Canadian importing distributor Gordie has been buying Glotz widgets for many years. He is also a race car enthusiast, and has attended the Indy 500 every year since 1972. Since each trip takes him past Glotz's Fort Wayne factory, he mixes business with pleasure by driving down in his truck and picking up a load of widgets on his way home. These sales are handled on an EXW basis. Shipments of widgets to Canada do not require export licenses, so there's no required export reporting. All Gordie needs is a commercial invoice and a copy of the blanket NAFTA certificate of origin. He even loads the truck himself, as he usually picks up the weekend following the race when Glotz's loading crew is not at work.

Proforma invoice EXW 3 is typical of what Gordie gets from Glotz before leaving Canada. It is similar to the kind Andre sends Otto, since both parties handle transportation, are willing to load their own trucks, and face no export clearance hurdles.

Riddle and Glotz
Riddle distributes Glotz's widgets throughout the Pacific Northwest. They usually purchase in truckload quantities, but occasionally require next day delivery to meet a customer's urgent requirements. Glotz normally provides proforma invoices as order acknowledgments to their large distributors to inform them when a shipment is leaving and what it contains and therefore help them balance their inventories. This procedure is followed even for small shipments.
Riddle has negotiated some excellent next-day delivery freight rates with a small package carrier. They always place urgently needed orders on an EXW basis, since they are arranging and paying for all transportation, and unlike larger shipments the driver loads his own truck. See Glotz's proforma invoice EXW 4.

Resinas de Oscar and Andre
Oscar is an importer of plastic molding compound used in widget production. Anticipating a huge price increase, he has purchased an excessively large quantity from a supplier outside the EU. Rather than immediately clearing it for import, he has stored it in a bonded warehouse. He has spent far too much on this, and needs to quickly sell it. Andre agreed to a rock bottom price and terms of EXW warehouse, from which he will clear the molding compound as needed. See proforma EXW 5

AMERICAN VIEWPOINT

International use
For reasons that are very obvious to Otto and any other foreign buyer, few U.S. export sales contracts are concluded on the EXW Incoterms® rule. Even buyers that have arranged "door-to-door" transportation and have forwarders willing to handle the export clearance obligation would encounter the problem of loading the collecting conveyance.

The United States has a policy whereby all exports are subject to some degree of control. Although other federal government agencies have some jurisdiction, the lion's share of export control is managed by the

United States Department of Commerce, Bureau of Industry & Security (BIS). For most items, it determines whether shipment of a given product to a given party in a given country for a given end use may be shipped without a license or a license exception. If an export license is required, it must be secured from BIS or other federal agency having jurisdiction before shipment can legally take place.
The Department of the Treasury, Office of Foreign Assets Control (OFAC) also has significant export control responsibility. So does the State Department Directorate of Defense Trade Controls (DDTC), which is merging its control list with Commerce's. These agencies maintain separate "bad guy" lists of parties and countries to which trade is restricted. Without some pretty sophisticated U.S. representation, foreign buyers would find it almost impossible to understand and comply with all these export regulations.

Until the Census Bureau's Foreign Trade Statistical Regulations (FTSR) were revised in early 2000s some U.S. exporters tried to used EXW to distance themselves from any export control compliance responsibility. The FTSR and subsequent Foreign Trade Regulations of 2008 prevent this by introducing the concept of U.S. Principal Party in Interest (USPPI), which includes EXW sellers. See the American Perspective chapter 24 for more information on export reporting.

Sometimes, a foreign buyer will ask a U.S. exporter to go beyond its EXW responsibility and handle export clearance. This can be risky for the exporter, as under EXW the seller has no control or even firsthand knowledge of any transportation. (Think of a buyer leaving the seller's loading dock in a taxi.) This could open the door for all manner of illegal diversion.

The EXW Incoterms® rule can also facilitate export diversion that does not violate regulations but may disrupt the seller's export distribution. Let's say a seller has cultivated a relationship with an excellent French importing distributor. This distributor is a textbook case of doing it right: places large orders frequently, never runs out of stock, pays correctly, aggressively promotes the line and provides excellent after-sale service. These efforts result in that brand being the most popular in France. The distributor's local competition would love to get their hands on the product, but the seller wisely supports the distributor and refuses to sell to anyone else in France. Enter a buyer with a huge EXW order for Paraguay, a country in which the exporter has no activity. Guess where the product really winds up. Guess whose distributor is furious.

Sellers should also be aware that the EXW rule does not obligate the buyer to export at all. Bogus export transactions could be diverted to the domestic market. This can be very disruptive for branded goods or those sold at substantial discount for export.

U.S. importers face mirror image problems, as most countries have export control regulations of their own. Additionally, countries with value added taxation (VAT) regimes typically forgive this sales tax for exports. Savvy buyers know this, and demand lower pricing from their suppliers. However, in order to obtain VAT relief, the foreign sellers must provide proof of export to their governments which can be difficult or impossible when they do not handle export clearance themselves.

Having explained how impractical EXW is for U.S. exports and imports, let me explain its importance as a basis for building towards more usable Incoterms® rules. The EXW price includes product and packaging only. (Sellers: be sure to include a separate line item price for any heroic export packing on your quotations.) Everything else is extra, including loading the collecting conveyance. By adding line items for additional services provided (like forwarding, pre-carriage, main carriage, on carriage, insurance, etc.), and graduating to a more appropriate rule, sellers can demonstrate what they are offering at what prices. Informed buyers appreciate such information.

Domestic use
EX Works can be appropriate for domestic transactions where there is no export clearance involved and loading can be done by someone other than the seller. Small package carriers immediately come to mind. There are also "self-loading" conveyances for situations like bulk commodity shipments (not to be confused

with vessel loading as covered by the FOB Incoterms® rule). Also, some types of product are withdrawn rather than loaded, such as from public warehouses or consignment inventories.

PROFORMA INVOICE

EXPORTER Les Widgets de France Rue John-Pierre Robin 12 Strasbourg FRANCE	**PROFORMA INVOICE #** EXW 1	**PROFORMA INVOICE DATE** September 30, 2020	
	PROFORMA VALIDITY DATE October 30, 2020	**EST'D SHIPMENT DATE** Tomorrow	
SOLD TO Widgets by Otto III Dean Haberkampstrasse Baden Baden GERMANY	**TERMS OF PAYMENT** Net 30 days		
	SHIPMENT/DELIVERY TERMS EXW Rue John-Pierre Robin 12, Strasbourg, France, Incoterms 2020		
SHIP TO Pick Up	**TITLE** Ownership transfers when payment is received by seller		

QUANTITY	UNITS	DESCRIPTION OF MERCHANDISE	UNIT PRICE	TOTAL
40	Each	Bleu widgets	€ 100.00	4000.00

LAW & DISPUTE RESOLUTION: The U.N. Convention on Contracts for the International Sale of Goods (1980) shall apply to this offer and any resulting contract. Any disputes will be resolved by binding arbitration services of the International Chamber of Commerce.	**MERCHANDISE TOTAL**	€ 4000.00
	GRAND TOTAL EXW Strasbourg	€ 4000.00

PROFORMA INVOICE

EXPORTER Glotz Industries Inc 1492 Columbus Boulevard Fort Wayne, Indiana 12345-6789 USA	**PROFORMA INVOICE #** EXW 2 **PROFORMA INVOICE DATE** September 30, 2020 **PROFORMA VALIDITY DATE** October 30, 2020 **EST'D SHIPMENT DATE** November 15, 2020
SOLD TO Widgets by Otto III Dean Haberkampstrasse Baden Baden GERMANY	**TERMS OF PAYMENT** Net 30 days **SHIPMENT/DELIVERY TERMS** EXW 1492 Columbus Blvd., Fort Wayne, Indiana, USA, Incoterms 2020
SHIP TO Pick Up	**TITLE** Ownership transfers when payment is received by seller

QUANTITY	UNITS	DESCRIPTION OF MERCHANDISE	UNIT PRICE	TOTAL
20	Each	Blue widgets	100.00	2000.00

LAW & DISPUTE RESOLUTION: The U.N. Convention on Contracts for the International Sale of Goods (1980) shall apply to this offer and any resulting contract. Any disputes will be resolved by binding arbitration services of the International Chamber of Commerce.	**MERCHANDISE TOTAL** Export Packing	**US$** 2000.00 123.00
	GRAND TOTAL EXW Fort Wayne	**US$** 2123.00

PROFORMA INVOICE

EXPORTER Glotz Industries Inc 1492 Columbus Boulevard Fort Wayne, Indiana 12345-6789 USA	**PROFORMA INVOICE #** EXW 3 **PROFORMA INVOICE DATE** May 25, 2020 **PROFORMA VALIDITY DATE** June 25, 2020 **EST'D SHIPMENT DATE** June 5, 2020
SOLD TO Gordie's Good Widgets 1 Carl Crewson Street North Bay, Ontario CANADA	**TERMS OF PAYMENT** Net 30 days **SHIPMENT/DELIVERY TERMS** EXW 1492 Columbus Blvd., Fort Wayne, Indiana, USA, Incoterms 2020
SHIP TO Pick Up	**TITLE** Ownership transfers when payment is received by seller

QUANTITY	UNITS	DESCRIPTION OF MERCHANDISE	UNIT PRICE	TOTAL
40	Each	Blue widgets	100.00	4000.00

LAW & DISPUTE RESOLUTION: The U.N. Convention on Contracts for the International Sale of Goods (1980) shall apply to this offer and any resulting contract. Any disputes will be resolved by binding arbitration services of the International Chamber of Commerce.	**MERCHANDISE TOTAL**	**US$** 4000.00
	GRAND TOTAL EXW Fort Wayne	**US$** 4000.00

PROFORMA INVOICE

SELLER
Glotz Industries Inc
1492 Columbus Boulevard
Fort Wayne, Indiana 12345-6789
USA

PROFORMA INVOICE #
EXW 4

PROFORMA INVOICE DATE
September 30, 2020

PROFORMA VALIDITY DATE
October 30, 2020

EST'D SHIPMENT DATE
October 8, 2020

SOLD TO
Riddle Enterprises
1066 Campbell Ct.
Seattle, Washington
USA

TERMS OF PAYMENT
Net 30 days

SHIPMENT/DELIVERY TERMS
EXW 1492 Columbus Boulevard, Fort Wayne, Indiana, USA, Incoterms 2020

SHIP TO
Pick Up

TITLE
Ownership transfers when payment is received by seller

QUANTITY	UNITS	DESCRIPTION OF MERCHANDISE	UNIT PRICE	TOTAL
4	Each	Blue widgets	89.00	356.00

LAW & DISPUTE RESOLUTION: The law of the state of Indiana shall apply to this offer and any resulting contract. Any disputes will be resolved by binding arbitration services of the American Arbitration Association.

MERCHANDISE TOTAL	US$ 356.00
GRAND TOTAL EXW Fort Wayne	**US$** 356.00

PROFORMA INVOICE

SELLER Resinas de Oscar Jean Claude Gamache 12 Le Havre, France	**PROFORMA INVOICE #** EXW 5 **PROFORMA INVOICE DATE** September 1, 2020 **PROFORMA VALIDITY DATE** September 20, 2020 **EST'D SHIPMENT DATE** On site
SOLD TO Les Widgets de France Rue John-Pierre Robin 12 Strasbourg France	**TERMS OF PAYMENT** Net 10 days **SHIPMENT/DELIVERY TERMS** EXW Free Trade Zone #12, area 272, Le Havre, Incoterms 2020
SHIP TO Located in Free Trade Zone #12, Le Havre	**TITLE** Ownership transfers when payment is received by seller

QUANTITY	UNITS	DESCRIPTION OF MERCHANDISE	UNIT PRICE	TOTAL
200,000	kilos	Grade C molding polymer	€ 7.00 / kg	€ 1,400,000.00

LAW & DISPUTE RESOLUTION: The law of France shall apply to this offer and any resulting contract. Any disputes will be resolved by binding arbitration services of the International Chamber of Commerce.	**MERCHANDISE TOTAL**	€ 1,400,000.00
	GRAND TOTAL EXW Free Trade Zone Le Havre	€ 1,400,000.00

CHAPTER 11 - F-GROUP RULES

There are three F-Group Incoterms®[20] rules: FCA, FAS ad FOB. FCA may be used for all transport modes while FAS and FOB are designed for use only when main carriage is done by vessel.

The main thing that F-Group rules have in common is that, with one unfortunate exception, the seller is not responsible for main carriage. This leaves main carriage to the buyer, which means that the buyer selects and contracts with the main carrier. It usually means that the buyer selects the freight forwarder as the roles of carrier and forwarder have blended to the point where they are almost indistinguishable. Therefore, for all three F-Group rules, the buyers are actually the shippers, at least for main and any subsequent carriage.

The above-mentioned unfortunate exception is a provision that the sellers and buyers may agree that the sellers handle transportation at the buyers' cost and risk. The kind of transportation is not specified but it presumably is main carriage. I strongly suggest that you do not go there. This creates a gray area and is out of step with the logic behind F-Group rules. If the parties want the seller to handle transportation, consider the C-Group rules (and be sure to include the freight cost in your price quotation). This writer has asked many experts for the difference between the F-Group exception and C-Group rules, and has received only one very limited reason. It is possible that sellers may wish to keep the freight cost confidential, and therefore would prefer a C-Group rule and provide freight prepaid but unrated transport documentation. By contrast, with an F-Group rule made under this exception, the buyers would be entitled to know the freight costs. While writing this book, I thought of another limited but possible reason which would apply only to the FOB rule, and only through employing some very circular logic. Interested readers should refer to the FOB chapter for details.

All F-Group rules are used in shipment contracts. Sellers deliver by handing over the contract goods to carriers somewhere on the sellers' side.

SELLERS

F-Group rules provide little advantage for sellers except possibly that there is less work involved than with more seller-friendly rules. F-Group rules increase the payment risk with document-driven payment terms by reducing the seller's control over the documentary process. Same goes for compliance risk, at least for items subject to enhanced export controls.

There is also a manageable conflict with the Census Bureau's Foreign Trade Regulations, at least as of this writing (July 2019). Under the F-Group rules, buyers normally handle main carriage and therefore normally appoint the freight forwarders. Census regulations state that a "routed transaction" occurs when buyers select freight forwarders, and that these forwarders should file the Electronic Export Information (EEI). However, such filing is part of "export clearance," which is a seller obligation under F-Group Incoterms® rules. There is a possible remedy, as Census' regulations permit foreign buyers to appoint anyone here to file the EEI, and this includes sellers. Request written authorization from the buyer to file the EEI, and with it in hand inform the buyer-appointed forwarder that you will be filing the EEI, and that you must have the required transport information in writing prior to export. Buyers normally agree. After all, export clearance is

[20] Incoterms® is a trademark of the International Chamber of Commerce, registered in several countries.

explicitly tasked in all F-Group rules, and as sellers are unlikely to charge for doing this while buyer-appointed forwarders normally do. Sellers benefit by filing not only through assured filing compliance but also access to the transportation information. This may facilitate their obtaining lower freight costs for future transactions, thereby steering them to the more seller-friendly C-Group rules.

BUYERS

F-Group transactions usually result from buyer's stronger price negotiation power with carriers or seller indifference. F-Group rules strongly favor informed buyers by providing control over main carriage. Frequent carrier selection results in lower negotiated freight costs for buyers, making continued F-Group use increasingly attractive. Where applicable, the Importer Security Filing (ISF) pre-shipment reporting requirements provide another reason for U.S. importers to use F-Group rules.

CHAPTER 12 - FREE CARRIER

Abbreviation: FCA
Transport mode: all
Contract type: shipment
Place: somewhere on the seller's side of any main carriage

Free Carrier (FCA) is the most versatile of the F-Group Incoterms[21]® rules. It can be used with any mode of transportation, and there are two possible alternatives, both on the seller's side of any main carriage:
either,
the place where shipment begins (often the seller's premises);
or,
anywhere else after pre-carriage on the seller's side.

AT THE PLACE WHERE SHIPMENT BEGINS

All the seller needs to do is have the contract goods suitably packaged at the agreed time, and promptly notify the buyer that they are ready. As the seller merely supplies the goods without any transportation arrangements, it falls to the buyer to make them. The seller is responsible for loading the collecting conveyance, and delivers by doing so. The seller must notify the buyer that either the carrier has picked up the goods or has failed to do so. The seller is also obligated to handle any export clearance.

ANYWHERE ELSE ON THE SELLER'S SIDE

In this situation, the seller provides pre-carriage to the agreed place. While the place could be any agreed place on the seller's side, for international use it is likely a buyer-appointed carrier's terminal or forwarder's warehouse. The seller is obligated to handle any export clearance. The FCA rule should not be used with a final destination, as the seller has no (main) carriage obligation under A4[22]. For both domestic and international use when the agreed place is anywhere other than the place where shipment begins, the seller is responsible for the condition of the contract goods, the transportation costs, and any transport security requirements until they get there. Once the delivering conveyance arrives, the seller has delivered. The seller is not responsible for unloading the delivering conveyance. The seller must also notify the buyer either that the goods have been delivered, or that the buyer-appointed party has failed to receive them.

The logic behind loading and unloading responds to the simple question: which party is best equipped to handle the task. The seller has the people and forklift equipment available to load when the place is its own premises. When it is another place, the party at that other place (for instance, a buyer-appointed carrier's terminal) would have the necessary people and equipment for unloading.

FCA is designed for delivery to occur on the seller's side of subsequent (main) carriage. The FCA rule is used for shipment contracts, and is not a substitute for an arrival contract rule like DPU, DAP or DDP. This is obvious when FCA is accompanied by the place where the shipment begins. Even when the accompanying place is elsewhere, the seller is handing over the goods to a buyer-appointed party for subsequent

---

[21] Incoterms® is a trademark of the International Chamber of Commerce, registered in several countries.

[22] Note: Although arranging for any main carriage is normally a buyer obligation, the parties sometimes agree that the seller take on this task for the buyer at the buyer's risk and cost. The resulting documentation would be a freight-prepaid transport document, with carriage arrangements made by the seller for the account of the buyer. The writer strongly advises against this option, and recommends that the parties instead consider CPT or CIP in such situations.

transportation. This is the reason A4 of the FCA rule states that the seller is not responsible for (main) carriage.

We will cover the two FCA possibilities separately with examples of each.

ON-BOARD VERSUS RECEIVED FOR SHIPMENT MARINE TRANSPORT DOCUMENT

Incoterms® 2020 rules attempt to address a documentary issue that frequently occurs when the FCA rule is used for containerized vessel shipments with letter of credit payment terms. Banks typically insist on presentation of a "clean on-board ocean bill of lading" in their letters of credit. Waterborne carriers will not issue on-board documentation prior to vessel loading. However, the delivery point with FCA is when the contract goods have been placed at the disposal of the carrier, which happens prior to vessel loading. The net result is that for FCA, sellers successful presentation under a letter of credit depends on a document reflecting activities that occur beyond the FCA delivery point. Risk for the condition of the contract goods has passed, but payment risk remains through documented vessel loading.

Banking experts were consulted, and their opinion is that the on-board requirement will remain.

In order to mitigate the risk to FCA sellers, provision was made under B6 Delivery / transport document that the parties may agree that the buyer must instruct the carrier to provide the seller with an on-board transport document at the buyer's cost and risk. Under A6, the seller would then be required to provide this document to the buyer, presumably as part of a letter of credit presentation. This would build some level of protection for the FCA seller into the sales-purchase contract.

This is a clever and well-intended step in the right direction. It does provide some leverage to the seller in dealing with a buyer-appointed carrier through its contract with the buyer. However, risks remain.

1. Since no marine carrier will issue an on-board document prematurely, sellers must wait until vessel loading to get it.
2. What happens if loss or damage occurs prior to vessel loading? Carriers cannot be expected to issue clean documentation for goods lost or damaged in pre-carriage.
3. A less likely situation could be a carrier refusal to release the document despite the buyer's instructions. The seller has no contract with the carrier, but presumably could take legal action against the buyer for breach of the sales contract.
4. Why are the parties using a letter of credit in the first place? If it is lack of confidence in the buyer's ability or willingness to pay, how much protection does the seller gain from a possible breach of contract action against the buyer?

These are not criticisms of the remedy, but underline the inherent risk of using any F-Group rules with letters of credit. C-Group rules are far safer for documentary compliance.

Incidentally, the new remedy applies to FCA only. FOB requires on-board documentation by definition. FAS does not task sellers with vessel loading, and bankers generally understand this venerable rule. With the C-Group rules, the seller contracts for carriage and therefore is in a position to require the carrier to provide appropriate documentation. Letters of credit are seldom appropriate with D-Group rules as they focus on arrival rather than shipment.

FCA + PLACE WHERE SHIPMENT BEGINS (OFTEN THE SELLER'S PREMISES)

This is what we really mean when we use the "F.O.B. Factory" term so beloved to Americans! The stipulated place is where transportation begins, often the seller's own premises. This should be described in geographic terms in as much detail as possible, including addresses, such as FCA 703 Tom Lange Boulevard, Holland, Ohio, Incoterms® 2020.

FCA + place where shipment begins works well when buyers have contracted for pre-carriage transportation or pick the goods up themselves, as sellers load the collecting conveyances.

International shipments are accommodated, since sellers are responsible for export clearance under this Incoterms® rule. Sellers need to exercise due diligence as they are not in a position to know the disposition of their shipments once they depart. Savvy U.S. exporters use the Census Bureau's FTRs to their advantage by obtaining written authorizations from their buyers to file the EEIs. They then insist that the buyer-appointed forwarders / carriers[23] provide the transportation information in writing prior to shipment to enable them to file. The buyers should have no reluctance to provide such authorizations, since under the FCA rule they have already agreed that the sellers should handle export clearance. In fact, any buyer reluctance should be treated with suspicion, as it would be contrary to the sales contract.

BUYER-SELLER RESPONSIBILITIES

The following is a short list of responsibilities.

1. **Goods and Payment**
   The seller must have the goods available when promised, suitably packaged, and must promptly notify the buyer that they are available for pickup. The seller must also notify the buyer if the collecting vehicle does not show up or fails to take the goods. The buyer must pay the seller. FCA may be used with all means of transport. For this reason, the seller's obligation to suitably package may largely depend upon the buyer making the seller aware of the transportation arrangements, particularly for international transactions. For instance, if the buyer gives the seller reason to believe that shipment will be made by air, and changes plans without the seller's knowledge, the seller would not know to provide the more robust packaging required for waterborne shipments.
2. **Loading the collecting conveyance**
   The seller is responsible for loading the collecting conveyance.
3. **Pre-carriage**
   The seller is not responsible. This presents no particular problem with domestic shipments. No particular problem for international shipments either, provided the buyer has a "door-to-somewhere" carriage contract or has a forwarder on the seller's side to arrange this. When this isn't the case, buyers could be put in an awkward situation of trying to arrange pre-carriage in foreign countries.
4. **Export clearance**
   This is a seller responsibility under this rule.
5. **Other hoops and hurdles**
   The seller is responsible for compliance with any transport security regulations through delivery, which in this case takes place where shipment begins. It must provide the buyer with any information on transport security regulations that it has in its possession. Since security regulations change often and vary from country to country and from one transport mode to another, Incoterms® rules

[23] The roles of carrier and forwarder have largely merged in today's transportation practices.

are limited to making the parties aware that they must be addressed. This is covered in A4-B4 and A7-B7.

6. **Insurance**
   Neither party is required to insure under FCA. However, common sense dictates otherwise, and insurance should be addressed outside of the rule. This is particularly important for buyers because the seller delivers prior to any transportation.
7. **Documentary implications**
   e. Commercial Documents: The seller should provide a commercial invoice, a packing list, and any other commercial documents cited in the sales contract.
   f. Transport Documents: The seller is required to provide proof of delivery but not necessarily a transport document. However, in order to prove delivery it may require the collecting conveyance to provide a receipt. Since the seller is required to load, a freight collect truck bill of lading prepared by the seller but signed by the driver is typical. If requested, the seller must also assist the buyer in obtaining a transport document at the buyer's cost and risk.
      Caution with using the new provision covering on-board marine transport documents when the agreed place is where shipment begins, i.e., prior to any pre-carriage. The documentary risk to the seller is proportionate to the time and distance between delivery (in this case loading the collecting vehicle) and vessel loading. See the FCA + Other Agreed Place section of this chapter for a realistic example of this new provision.
   g. Export Control Documentation: The seller is obligated to handle export clearance under this Incoterms® rule. In a routed transaction, as the USPPI the seller is obligated at a minimum to provide company and product specific information to the buyer-appointed agent for EEI filing. Proactive sellers who obtain buyer authorizations and file the EEIs will have an electronic record of filing. Note: for U.S. exports of reportable items, the value for EEI filing shall be the value of the goods in US dollars at the port, airport or land border of export (or the cost if not sold). See 15CFR Part 30.6(a)(17). Estimates are permitted.
   h. Import Entry Documentation: This is a buyer obligation. However, A7 requires the seller to provide assistance at the buyer's request, risk and cost.
8. **Payment terms considerations**
   By definition, the buyer must arrange for pick-up at the stipulated place under this version of the FCA Incoterms® rule. It then follows that the seller must be prepared to turn the goods over at that place. This means there's often no way to use documents to restrict possession of the goods. One possibility is the new on-board marine transport document provision. It is also possible that a buyer-appointed forwarder's receipt could be used to trigger a letter of credit. A negotiable freight collect received for shipment multimodal transportation document is another possibility for letters of credit and documentary collections. However, in all cases, as the seller is not contracting for carriage, the risk exists that the buyer-appointed carrier or forwarder may not follow any seller-provided instructions, and may refuse to provide the needed document to the seller. Therefore, open account (or even payment in advance) terms are commonly used.

STORY LINE

Otto and Andre

Otto is a young importer of widgets located in Baden Baden, Germany. Andre is Otto's French widget supplier, located in Strasbourg, France, quite near the German border. Whenever Otto sends a common carrier truck, the parties agree to use the FCA Incoterms® rule accompanied by the address of Andre's factory as shown in Andre's proforma invoice FCA 1. Otto has negotiated an excellent freight rate. Andre prepares Otto's order for shipment and loads the truck when it arrives. All carriage is handled by the same trucking company. There are no export or import clearance formalities between France and Germany as both are EU members.

Otto and Glotz
Otto wishes to purchase from Glotz Industries, a Fort Wayne widget manufacturer. Although the parties have enjoyed a longstanding relationship, neither has access to the way business had been conducted in the past. Both are literally starting from scratch. As shown in proforma invoice FCA 2, Glotz requoted using the FCA Incoterms® rule after Otto rejected Glotz's EXW proposal. This relieved Otto of any loading or export clearance obligation, but the idea of making transportation arrangements from a factory in an unknown part of a foreign country was still too much for Otto to accept. He again requested Glotz to assume more of the transaction burden by quoting under a different Incoterms® rule. We'll see the results in subsequent chapters.

Gordie and Glotz
This is the way Gordie normally purchases when he is not visiting Indiana. He has negotiated an excellent door-to-door freight rate. Because of cabotage agreements between the U.S. and Canada, the same truck line that picks up at Glotz's factory delivers at Gordie's warehouse. See Glotz's proforma invoice FCA 3. This situation parallels Otto and Andre above.

Riddle and Glotz
Similar to Otto and Andre and Gordie and Glotz above. See Glotz's proforma invoice FCA 4

Andre and Jamal
Jamal has a small widget importing company in Casablanca, Morocco. He had been placing frequent small orders with Andre for years on FCA Andre's premises and open account payment terms. They communicate well in French and have developed a trusting relationship. See Andre's proforma invoice FCA 5.

FCA + OTHER AGREED PLACE ON SELLER"S SIDE

This version of the FCA Incoterms® rule works well when the seller delivers to a location other than its premises and on the seller's side of main carriage. Examples of such places include a buyer-appointed carrier, a buyer-appointed forwarder or a buyer-appointed container consolidator. When used for international sales we say "seller's side" to mean the seller's side of subsequent (main) carriage, a location often in the seller's own country. Because FCA A4 specifies that the seller has no carriage obligation,[24] it should not be used with a location on the buyer's side. For international use, the seller arranges for pre-carriage transportation to the agreed place, and remains responsible for the condition of the contract goods until they arrive there. Delivery occurs when the delivering conveyance arrives at the agreed place, not unloaded. The reason is that the buyer-appointed carrier, forwarder, etc. would normally have people and equipment at its disposal to unload at its premises.

The place should be described in geographic terms in as much detail as possible, including addresses, such as Transair Lines, Building 2, Toledo Express Airport, Incoterms® 2020.

International shipments are accommodated since sellers are responsible for export clearance under this Incoterms® rule. Exporters need to exercise due diligence as they are not in a position to know the disposition of their shipments once they are delivered. However, as they are usually bringing them to a buyer-appointed carrier or forwarder, they are a transport leg closer to the actual export than is the case with EXW or FCA + place where shipment begins. It should be fairly easy to check the reputation of the carrier or forwarder. Savvy U.S. exporters use the Census Bureau's FTRs to their advantage by obtaining written authorizations from their buyers to file the EEIs. They then insist that the buyer-appointed forwarders / carriers[25] provide the transportation information in writing prior to shipment to enable them to file. The buyers should have no reluctance to provide authorizations since under the FCA rule they have already agreed that the sellers should handle export clearance. In fact, any buyer reluctance should be treated with suspicion as it would be contrary to the sales contract.

This FCA alternative works well when sellers provide or contract for pre-carriage transportation. As mentioned at the start of this chapter, FCA should not be used as an arrival contract rule such as DAP, DPU or DDP.

BUYER-SELLER RESPONSIBILITIES

The following is a short list of responsibilities.

1. **Goods and Payment**
   The seller must have the goods available when promised, suitably packaged, must promptly notify the buyer that they are ready, and must transport them to the agreed place on the seller's side. The seller must then advise the buyer either that the goods have been delivered or that the buyer-appointed party refused to take them. The buyer must pay the seller.
   FCA may be used with all means of transport. For this reason, the seller's obligation to suitably package may largely depend upon the buyer making the seller aware of the subsequent transportation arrangements, particularly for export. This may be obvious because of the agreed delivery place (seaport, airport, container consolidator, etc.).
2. **Loading and unloading**

[24] See footnote 2.

[25] See footnote 3.

The seller is responsible for loading the pre-carrying conveyance, but the buyer is responsible for unloading.

3. **Pre-carriage**
   This is a seller responsibility under this FCA version.
4. **Export clearance**
   This is a seller responsibility under this rule.
5. **Other hoops and hurdles**
   The seller is responsible for compliance with any transport security regulations through delivery, which in this case takes place after pre-carriage but prior to unloading. It must provide the buyer with any information on transport security regulations that it has in its possession. Since security regulations change often and vary from country to country and from one transport mode to another, Incoterms® rules are limited to making the parties aware that they must be addressed. This is covered in A4-B4 and A7-B7.
6. **Insurance**
   Neither party is required to insure under FCA. However, common sense dictates otherwise, and insurance should be addressed outside of the rule. Sellers are at risk through pre-carriage. Buyers are at risk thereafter. For vessel shipments, insurance coverage from the point that that the goods are handed over to the buyer-appointed carrier through vessel loading (so-called FAS-FOB coverage) can be important to sellers who require on-board documentation.
7. **Documentary implications**
   a. Commercial Documents: The seller should provide a commercial invoice, a packing list, and any other commercial documents cited in the sales contract.
   b. Transport Documents: The seller should provide evidence that the contract goods were received at the agreed place. If requested, the seller must also assist the buyer in obtaining a transport document at the buyer's cost and risk.
      Note the new provision covering on-board marine transport documents. The seller's risk for the condition of the goods ends when they are handed over to the buyer-appointed carrier. For vessel shipments under this rule this would probably be at a port location. However, on board documentation will not become available until and unless the goods are loaded. Therefore, sellers face a documentary risk[26] through vessel loading by a buyer appointed carrier. If all goes well, the buyer-appointed forwarder will provide the seller with the on board transport document. The seller must then provide it to the buyer so that the buyer can collect the contract goods from the carrier on arrival. This is usually done through banking channels as with letters of credit or documentary collections.
   c. Export Control Documentation: The seller is obligated to handle export clearance under this Incoterms® rule. In a routed transaction, as the USPPI the seller is obligated at a minimum to provide company and product specific information to the buyer-appointed agent for EEI filing. Proactive sellers who obtain buyer authorizations and file the EEIs will have an electronic record of filing. Note: for U.S. exports of reportable items, the value for EEI filing shall be the value of the goods in US dollars at the port, airport or land border of export (or the cost if not sold). See 15CFR Part 30.6(a)(17). Estimates are permitted.
   d. Import Entry Documentation: This is a buyer obligation. However, A7 requires the seller to provide assistance at the buyer's request, risk and cost.
8. **Payment terms considerations**
   By definition, the seller must arrange for delivery at the stipulated place under this version of the FCA Incoterms® rule. It then follows that the seller must be prepared to turn the goods over at that place. This means there's often no way to use documents to restrict possession of the goods. One possibility is the new on-board marine transport document provision. It is also possible that a buyer-appointed forwarder's receipt could be used to trigger a letter of credit. A negotiable freight collect received for shipment multimodal transportation document is another possibility for letters of credit and documentary collections. However, in all cases, as the seller is not contracting for carriage, the

[26] Documentary risk usually equates to payment risk with letter of credit payment terms.

risk exists that the buyer-appointed carrier or forwarder may not follow any seller or even buyer provided instructions, and may refuse to provide the needed document to the seller. Therefore, open account (or even payment in advance) terms are commonly used.

STORY LINE

Otto and Andre

Otto is a young importer of widgets located in Baden Baden, Germany. Andre is Otto's French widget supplier, located in Strasbourg, France, quite near the German border. Because the two places are so close to each other, they never use subsequent carriers, and therefore do not use this FCA version.

Otto and Glotz

Otto wishes to purchase from Glotz Industries, a Fort Wayne widget manufacturer. Both are literally starting from scratch. As shown in proforma invoice FCA 6, Glotz agreed to arrange and pay for pre-carriage to an international carrier at O'Hare airport. This relieved Otto of any loading or export clearance obligation as well as transportation in the U.S. All he has to do is arrange main carriage, import clearance and on-carriage which he should be able to do from Germany. The question is, at what cost. Otto replied that this quotation was being considered, but that he would appreciate Glotz's shopping around for an air freight quotation. This will bring us to the CPT chapter.

Gordie and Glotz

Because of cabotage agreements between the U.S. and Canada, the same truck line that picks up at Glotz's factory delivers at Gordie's warehouse. For this reason, Gordie never uses this FCA version.
This situation parallels Otto and Andre above.

Jerry and Glotz

Jerry Prieto imports Glotz's widgets for use in his Monterrey battery factory. As shown in proforma FCA 7, he always uses this FCA version, specifying his forwarder's Laredo Texas warehouse as the location. There are several reasons for this. First, Mexican import regulations[27] require filing of all pertinent information and payment of duty before the "pedimento" (permission to import) is issued. This can take time. To accommodate this, many border forwarders offer warehousing and customs brokerage services on both sides. Next, although it is possible to get "door-to-door" freight rates, there is a physical change of equipment at the border. Finally, many U.S. exporters are not comfortable with transit risk within Mexico.

Riddle and Glotz

As a large distributor, Riddle is constantly receiving different sized shipments by different means. Ideally, they prefer to order monthly and in full truckload quantities. Very small urgently needed shipments travel next-day by small package carriers. There's a third alternative; less-than-truckload shipments that are not urgent enough for small package delivery but cannot await the usual monthly truckload shipment. Riddle has another supplier in South Bend, Indiana, from which it orders weekly truckload shipments. As shown in proforma FCA 8, it sometimes asks Glotz to deliver there for consolidation and subsequent transportation to Seattle.

Andre and Jamal

Jamal has a small widget importing company in Casablanca, Morocco. He had been placing frequent small orders with Andre for years on FCA Andre's premises and open account payment terms. They communicate well in French and have developed a trusting relationship. Jamal obtained a huge government order for a full container load, far above his normal requirements. The fact that it was for the government enabled him to have a letter of credit issued in Andre's favor, payable at Andre's bank. The transaction began as usual, with

---

[27] As of this writing under the NAFTA. The USMCA may expedite Mexican import clearance times.

the Incoterms® rule to be FCA Andre's premises, and Jamal's forwarder to arrange door-to-port transportation. However, like many banks, Jamal's insisted on presentation of a clean on-board freight collect ocean bill of lading consigned to order and blank endorsed. Because of the ongoing relationship, and impressed that Jamal was able to have such a large letter of credit issued, Andre accepted the documentary risk. However, because of the large amount and huge reliance on the performance of a buyer-appointed carrier, Andre preferred to contract for pre-carriage. They agreed to depart from their normal practice and change the place from Andre's premises to FCA Marseilles. They further agreed **in the sales contract** that Jamal's forwarder would make the on-board document available to Andre immediately after vessel loading, and that Andre would then promptly present it at BNP bank for payment. Speed was needed, as the transit time is short. Everyone did as promised, and the gray area between delivery and vessel loading at Marseilles was successfully bridged. See Andre's proforma invoice FCA 9.

AMERICAN VIEWPOINT TO BOTH VERSIONS

INTERNATIONAL USE

While the Incoterms® rule tasks the seller with export clearance, this can be at odds with local regulations.

Routed transactions[28]: For U.S. exports, the Census Bureau's Foreign Trade Regulations require the party appointed by the buyer to handle the export to file the Electronic Export Information (EEI). This usually translates to a buyer-appointed forwarder (or carrier as their roles are increasingly becoming interchangeable). The seller, known as the United States Principal Party in Interest (USPPI), is required to provide this party with its company and product specific information needed to file the EEI. In return, the USPPI is entitled only to written confirmation from this service provider of the information it provided. The USPPI has no right to the transportation information in this situation as the EEI is confidential between the filer and Census.

As mentioned earlier and explained in more detail in the American Perspective chapter 24, there is relief for exporters that prefer to file their EEIs in routed transactions rather than trusting service providers over which they have no control. An additional payoff is access to the transportation information. Savvy sellers use this to help their forwarders obtain lower freight costs and better service in order to gain control of future shipments.

There are a few other potential seller risks with all F-Group rules that stem from the buyer's contracting for main carriage with the carrier. This normally means that the buyer also appoints the forwarder. Both of these service providers would therefore follow instructions from the buyer rather than any they receive from the seller. This opens the possibility of diversion which could be illegal shipment to a prohibited party or country. More likely would be commercial diversion to a non-restricted party or country other than the destination understood by the seller. Depending on the product, doing so may or may not violate export regulations, but in any case could seriously compromise the seller's distribution arrangements.

As mentioned throughout this chapter, seller access to transportation documents could present a problem, particularly with document-driven payment terms. Don't be surprised to receive letters of credit calling for freight collect "on board ocean bills of lading" for an FCA transaction, extending the beneficiary's risk through vessel loading. Many banks simply will not accept a "received for shipment" document, regardless of the fact that this agrees with the seller's FCA Incoterms® obligation. Others confuse the "on board-ness" with consignment instructions. (It is perfectly possible to have a negotiable received for shipment marine transportation document.) As the buyer is contracting for main carriage, the seller who is beneficiary of such a letter of credit would be at risk for the loading operations of a carrier it did not choose and may never have

[28] As of this writing, Census is working on possible revisions to the routed transaction rules.

chosen. For this reason the new on-board document option was added to the A6 – B6 Delivery / transport document task line.

Another drawback is that each shipment made under F-Group Incoterms® rules is one more that isn't counted to the seller's credit in negotiating shippers' agreements. Service providers respect VOLUME above all. Shippers that control many shipments have, do, and always will pay lower freight costs and get better service than do less frequent shippers. Since the shipper is the party contracting for transportation with the carrier, the buyer is actually the shipper under F-Group rules.

U.S. importers do well with FCA. As opposed to EXW, the fact that export clearance is a seller obligation makes it easier for sellers in countries with value added tax to claim refunds, which may result in lower pricing. Also, U.S. import duty is not payable on freight to get here, so the FCA price is often the dutiable value. Freight cost savings and superior carrier service accrue to buyers who control enough shipments to become large shippers. Finally, the Importer Security Filing (ISF) rule holds importers responsible for filing detailed information with Customs prior to vessel loading for many waterborne import shipments. Controlling the overseas forwarder really helps compliance.

Domestic use

FCA presents no problem for purely domestic transactions.

PROFORMA INVOICE

EXPORTER Les Widgets de France Rue John-Pierre Robin 12 Strasbourg FRANCE	**PROFORMA INVOICE #** FCA 1	**PROFORMA INVOICE DATE** September 30, 2020
	PROFORMA VALIDITY DATE October 30, 2020	**EST'D SHIPMENT DATE** October 4, 2020
SOLD TO Widgets by Otto III Dean Haberkampstrasse Baden Baden GERMANY	**TERMS OF PAYMENT** Net 30 days	
	SHIPMENT/DELIVERY TERMS FCA Rue John-Pierre Robin 12, Strasbourg, France, Incoterms 2020	
SHIP TO Pick Up	**TITLE** Ownership transfers when payment is received by seller	

QUANTITY	UNITS	DESCRIPTION OF MERCHANDISE	UNIT PRICE	TOTAL
40	Each	Bleu widgets	€ 100.00	4000.00

LAW & DISPUTE RESOLUTION: The U.N. Convention on Contracts for the International Sale of Goods (1980) shall apply to this offer and any resulting contract. Any disputes will be resolved by binding arbitration services of the International Chamber of Commerce.	**MERCHANDISE TOTAL**	**€** 4000.00
	GRAND TOTAL FCA Strasbourg	**€** 4000.00

PROFORMA INVOICE

EXPORTER Glotz Industries Inc 1492 Columbus Boulevard Fort Wayne, Indiana 12345-6789 USA	**PROFORMA INVOICE #** FCA 2 **PROFORMA INVOICE DATE** October 5, 2020 **PROFORMA VALIDITY DATE** November 5, 2020 **EST'D SHIPMENT DATE** November 1, 2020
SOLD TO Widgets by Otto III Dean Haberkampstrasse Baden Baden GERMANY	**TERMS OF PAYMENT** Net 30 days **SHIPMENT/DELIVERY TERMS** FCA 1492 Columbus Blvd., Fort Wayne, Indiana, USA, Incoterms 2020
SHIP TO Pick Up	**TITLE** Ownership transfers when payment is received by seller

QUANTITY	UNITS	DESCRIPTION OF MERCHANDISE	UNIT PRICE	TOTAL
20	Each	Blue widgets	100.00	2000.00

LAW & DISPUTE RESOLUTION: The U.N. Convention on Contracts for the International Sale of Goods (1980) shall apply to this offer and any resulting contract. Any disputes will be resolved by binding arbitration services of the International Chamber of Commerce.	**MERCHANDISE TOTAL** Export Packing	**US$** 2000.00 123.00
	GRAND TOTAL FCA Fort Wayne	**US$** 2123.00

PROFORMA INVOICE

EXPORTER Glotz Industries Inc 1492 Columbus Boulevard Fort Wayne, Indiana 12345-6789 USA	**PROFORMA INVOICE #** FCA 3 **PROFORMA INVOICE DATE** September 30, 2020 **PROFORMA VALIDITY DATE** October 30, 2020 **EST'D SHIPMENT DATE** October 8, 2020
SOLD TO Gordie's Good Widgets 1 Carl Crewson Street North Bay, Ontario CANADA	**TERMS OF PAYMENT** Net 30 days **SHIPMENT/DELIVERY TERMS** FCA 1492 Columbus Blvd., Fort Wayne, Indiana, USA, Incoterms 2020
SHIP TO Pick Up	**TITLE** Ownership transfers when payment is received by seller

QUANTITY	UNITS	DESCRIPTION OF MERCHANDISE	UNIT PRICE	TOTAL
40	Each	Blue widgets	100.00	4000.00

LAW & DISPUTE RESOLUTION: The U.N. Convention on Contracts for the International Sale of Goods (1980) shall apply to this offer and any resulting contract. Any disputes will be resolved by binding arbitration services of the International Chamber of Commerce.	**MERCHANDISE TOTAL**	**US$** 4000.00
	GRAND TOTAL FCA Fort Wayne	**US$** 4000.00

PROFORMA INVOICE

SELLER Glotz Industries Inc 1492 Columbus Boulevard Fort Wayne, Indiana 12345-6789 USA	**PROFORMA INVOICE #** FCA 4 **PROFORMA INVOICE DATE** September 30, 2020 **PROFORMA VALIDITY DATE** October 30, 2020 **EST'D SHIPMENT DATE** October 8, 2020
SOLD TO Riddle Enterprises 1066 Campbell Ct. Seattle, Washington USA	**TERMS OF PAYMENT** Net 30 days **SHIPMENT/DELIVERY TERMS** FCA 1492 Columbus Boulevard, Fort Wayne, Indiana, USA, Incoterms 2020
SHIP TO Pick Up	**TITLE** Ownership transfers when payment is received by seller

QUANTITY	UNITS	DESCRIPTION OF MERCHANDISE	UNIT PRICE	TOTAL
450	Each	Blue widgets	89.00	40,50.00

LAW & DISPUTE RESOLUTION: The law of the state of Indiana shall apply to this offer and any resulting contract. Any disputes will be resolved by binding arbitration services of the American Arbitration Association.	**MERCHANDISE TOTAL**	**US$** 40,050.00
	GRAND TOTAL FCA Fort Wayne	**US$** 40,050.00

PROFORMA INVOICE

EXPORTER Les Widgets de France Rue Jean-Pierre Robin 12 Strasbourg FRANCE	**PROFORMA INVOICE #** FCA 5
	PROFORMA INVOICE DATE September 30, 2020
	PROFORMA VALIDITY DATE October 30, 2020
	EST'D SHIPMENT DATE October 5, 2020
SOLD TO Jamal Widgets 2 Boulevard Sidney Greenstreet Casablanca MOROCCO	**TERMS OF PAYMENT** Net 30 jours
	SHIPMENT/DELIVERY TERMS FCA Rue Jean-Pierre Robin 12, Strasbourg
SHIP TO Pick up	**TITLE** Ownership transfers when payment is received by seller

QUANTITY	UNITS	DESCRIPTION OF MERCHANDISE	UNIT PRICE	TOTAL
40	Each	Bleu widgets	€100.00	€4,000.00

LAW & DISPUTE RESOLUTION: The U.N. Convention on Contracts for the International Sale of Goods (1980) shall apply to this offer and any resulting contract. Any disputes will be resolved by binding arbitration services of the International Chamber of Commerce.	**MERCHANDISE TOTAL**	€4,000.00
	GRAND TOTAL FCA Strasbourg	€4,000.00

PROFORMA INVOICE

EXPORTER Glotz Industries Inc 1492 Columbus Boulevard Fort Wayne, Indiana 12345-6789 USA	**PROFORMA INVOICE #** FCA 6 **PROFORMA INVOICE DATE** October 7, 2020 **PROFORMA VALIDITY DATE** November 7, 2020 **EST'D SHIPMENT DATE** November 1, 2020
SOLD TO Widgets by Otto III Dean Haberkampstrasse Baden Baden GERMANY	**TERMS OF PAYMENT** Net 30 days **SHIPMENT/DELIVERY TERMS** FCA Air America Terminal 2, O'Hare Airport, Chicago, IL, USA, Incoterms 2020
SHIP TO Air America Terminal 2, O'Hare Airport, Chicago, IL, USA	**TITLE** Ownership transfers when payment is received by seller

QUANTITY	UNITS	DESCRIPTION OF MERCHANDISE	UNIT PRICE	TOTAL
20	Each	Blue widgets	100.00	2000.00

LAW & DISPUTE RESOLUTION: The U.N. Convention on Contracts for the International Sale of Goods (1980) shall apply to this offer and any resulting contract. Any disputes will be resolved by binding arbitration services of the International Chamber of Commerce.	**MERCHANDISE TOTAL** Export Packing Pre carriage	**US$** 2000.00 123.00 138.00
	GRAND TOTAL FCA O'Hare Airport	**US$** 2261.00

PROFORMA INVOICE

EXPORTER Glotz Industries Inc 1492 Columbus Boulevard Fort Wayne, Indiana 12345-6789 USA	**PROFORMA INVOICE #** FCA 7 **PROFORMA INVOICE DATE** September 30, 2020 **PROFORMA VALIDITY DATE** October 30, 2020 **EST'D SHIPMENT DATE** October 15, 2020
SOLD TO Baterias de Monterrey SA 55 Cantu Plaza Monterrey, NL, MEXICO	**TERMS OF PAYMENT** Net 30 days **SHIPMENT/DELIVERY TERMS** FCA 1836 Sam Houston Dr., Laredo, Texas, USA, Incoterms 2020
SHIP TO Rapido y Corecto Forwarding 1836 Sam Houston Dr. Laredo, Texas USA	**TITLE** Ownership transfers when payment is received by seller

QUANTITY	UNITS	DESCRIPTION OF MERCHANDISE	UNIT PRICE	TOTAL
40	Each	Blue widgets	100.00	4000.00

LAW & DISPUTE RESOLUTION: The U.N. Convention on Contracts for the International Sale of Goods (1980) shall apply to this offer and any resulting contract. Any disputes will be resolved by binding arbitration services of the International Chamber of Commerce.	**MERCHANDISE TOTAL** Pre carriage	**US$** 4000.00 872.00
	GRAND TOTAL FCA Laredo, Texas	**US$** 4872.00

PROFORMA INVOICE

SELLER Glotz Industries Inc 1492 Columbus Boulevard Fort Wayne, Indiana 12345-6789 USA	**PROFORMA INVOICE #** FCA 8 **PROFORMA INVOICE DATE** September 30, 2020 **PROFORMA VALIDITY DATE** October 30, 2020 **EST'D SHIPMENT DATE** October 8, 2020
SOLD TO Riddle Enterprises 1066 Campbell Ct. Seattle, Washington USA	**TERMS OF PAYMENT** Net 30 days **SHIPMENT/DELIVERY TERMS** FCA 1 Touchdown Dr, South Bend, Indiana, USA, Incoterms 2020
SHIP TO Riddle Enterprises c/o Othersupplier Inc 1 Touchdown Dr South Bend, Indiana, USA	**TITLE** Ownership transfers when payment is received by seller

QUANTITY	UNITS	DESCRIPTION OF MERCHANDISE	UNIT PRICE	TOTAL
14	Each	Blue widgets	100.00	1400.00

LAW & DISPUTE RESOLUTION: The law of the state of Indiana shall apply to this offer and any resulting contract. Any disputes will be resolved by binding arbitration services of the American Arbitration Association.	**MERCHANDISE TOTAL** Pre carriage	**US$** 1400.00 82.00
	GRAND TOTAL FCA South Bend	**US$** 1482.00

PROFORMA INVOICE

EXPORTER Les Widgets de France Rue Jean-Pierre Robin 12 Strasbourg FRANCE	**PROFORMA INVOICE #** FCA 9	**PROFORMA INVOICE DATE** September 30, 2020
	PROFORMA VALIDITY DATE October 30, 2020	**EST'D SHIPMENT DATE** October 24, 2020
SOLD TO Jamal Widgets 2 Boulevard Sidney Greenstreet Casablanca MOROCCO	**TERMS OF PAYMENT** Irrevocable letter of credit at sight through BNP Paribas, Strasbourg Branch	
	SHIPMENT/DELIVERY TERMS FCA CGM terminal, Marseilles Port	
SHIP TO CGM terminal, Marseilles Port	**TITLE** Ownership transfers when payment is received by seller	

QUANTITY	UNITS	DESCRIPTION OF MERCHANDISE	UNIT PRICE	TOTAL
4,000	Each	Bleu widgets	€88.00	€352,000.00

LAW & DISPUTE RESOLUTION: The U.N. Convention on Contracts for the International Sale of Goods (1980) shall apply to this offer and any resulting contract. Any disputes will be resolved by binding arbitration services of the International Chamber of Commerce.	**MERCHANDISE TOTAL** Container loading Pre carriage	€352,000.00 €870.00 €2,600.00
	GRAND TOTAL FCA Marseilles	€355,470.00

CHAPTER 13 - FREE ALONGSIDE SHIP

Abbreviation: FAS
Transport mode: vessel only
Contract type: shipment
Place: next to a buyer-appointed vessel at the agreed port on the seller's side

Free Alongside Ship (FAS) is a venerable marine-only Incoterms®[29] rule. Its practical use is generally limited to non-containerized waterborne shipments where the buyer contracts not only for main carriage but for vessel loading as well ("liner-in"). It can also be used in lighterage situations, where the port is too shallow to accommodate deep draft vessels and the receiving vessel is geared[30].

A4 of the FAS rule states that the seller is not tasked with providing carriage. However, the place is next to a buyer-appointed vessel, and the seller must get the goods there in order to deliver. The "no carriage" refers to main carriage here.

FAS reflects the way most cargo was handled prior to containerization. Ports were little more than collections of piers to which outbound cargo was delivered. Nowadays, modern container ports are very secure areas, and outbound cargo is normally handed over some distance from the ships. Still, there are situations where FAS is appropriate:

- with vessel chartering, where the buyer handles loading and main carriage, as is common in commodity trades or with break-bulk shipments of project cargo,
- where port rules define "along side" to be somewhere other than directly next to a vessel, such as the "Antwerp Rules,[31]"
- with lighterage[32], where ships are loaded from smaller vessels rather from piers,
- with containers at small or less developed ports when vessels have loading capability,
- when the goods have been sold after having been delivered alongside the ship.

It has probably occurred to you that FCA + the appropriate place could be substituted for every one of these situations. However, FAS is found in numerous industry-specific legacy contracts used every day.

The FAS rule is used for shipment contracts as the seller delivers when the goods arrive at the agreed place at the agreed port within the agreed time frame.

The seller must also notify the buyer either that the goods have been delivered or that the buyer-appointed carrier failed to receive them.

The location within the port should be described in geographic terms in as much detail as possible. With charter vessels, timing is extremely important because of the costs of needlessly tying up an entire vessel. Conversely, there are significant costs and risks in having goods arrive prematurely at a port awaiting the vessel. Sellers, buyers and carriers should work closely to coordinate the ship's arrival and the delivery of the goods.

Sellers are responsible for export clearance under this Incoterms® rule. Exporters need to exercise due diligence as they are not in a position to know the disposition of their shipments once they have been delivered. However, as they are bringing the goods to a buyer-appointed vessel, they are a transport leg

---

[29] Incoterms® is a trademark of the International Chamber of Commerce, registered in several countries.

[30] A "geared" vessel is one with lifting capability, i.e. a crane.

[31] Rules particular to the Port of Antwerp that define "alongside" in a distinctive manner.

[32] Ship to ship lighterage has become common in the petroleum industry because of ultra large crude tankers (ULCCs) that are too large for ports near some oil producing regions. These are covered by industry-specific contracts and government regulation, so we will avoid using them and stick to more basic examples.

closer to the actual export than is the case with EXW or FCA + seller's premises. Savvy U.S. exporters use the Census Bureau's FTRs to their advantage by obtaining written authorizations from their buyers to file the EEIs. They then insist that the buyer-appointed forwarders and carriers[33] provide the transportation information in writing prior to shipment to enable them to file. The buyers should have no reluctance to provide authorizations since under the FAS rule they have already agreed that the sellers handle export clearance. In fact, any buyer reluctance should be treated with suspicion as it would be contrary to the sales contract.

A2 of the FAS rule also accommodates sales of goods that have already been delivered. This is intended to facilitate the use of this rule in commodity trade, where goods are commonly sold while in transit (so called "string sales").

Note: Although arranging for any main carriage is strictly speaking a buyer obligation, sellers may agree take on this task for the buyers at the buyers' risk and cost. This is the unfortunate exception to the A4 carriage task. The resulting documentation would be a freight-prepaid transport document, with carriage arrangements made by the seller for the account of the buyer.

BUYER-SELLER RESPONSIBILITIES

The following is a short list of responsibilities.

1. **Goods and Payment**
   The seller must have the goods available when promised, suitably packaged, and must transport them to the agreed place at the agreed port on the seller's side. The buyer must pay the seller.
2. **Loading and unloading**
   The seller is responsible for placing the goods alongside the ship.
3. **Pre-carriage**
   This is a seller responsibility under this rule.
4. **Export clearance**
   This is a seller responsibility under this rule.
5. **Other hoops and hurdles**
   The seller is responsible for compliance with any transport security regulations through delivery. The parties must work together on cargo security information. Since security regulations change often and vary from country to country and from one transport mode to another, Incoterms® rules are limited to making the parties aware that they must be addressed. This is covered in A4-B4 and A7-B7.
6. **Insurance**
   Neither party is required to insure under FAS. However, common sense dictates otherwise, and insurance should be addressed outside of the rule. Sellers are at risk until the goods are delivered next to the vessel (check with your insurers about FAS/FOB coverage). Buyers are at risk thereafter.
7. **Documentary implications**
   a. Commercial Documents: The seller should provide a commercial invoice, a packing list, and any other commercial documents cited in the sales contract.
   b. Transport Documents: The seller should provide evidence that the contract goods were delivered to the agreed place. For charter vessel shipments this could be a mate's receipt. However, for shipments made on liner-in terms there is no specific document. A dock receipt might do, provided it indicates that the goods were placed next to the agreed vessel at the agreed place and port within the agreed time. Same for any other "received for shipment" marine transport

[33] The roles of carrier and forwarder have largely merged in today's transportation practice, with chartering as a possible exception.

document. Most do not provide that level of detail. On the other hand, since the seller is not responsible for vessel loading, an "on board" document would be inappropriate.

c. Export Control Documentation: The seller is obligated to handle export clearance under this Incoterms® rule. In a routed transaction, as the USPPI the seller is obligated at a minimum to provide company and product specific information to the buyer-appointed agent for EEI filing. Proactive sellers who obtain buyer authorizations and file the EEIs will have an electronic record of filing. Note: for U.S. exports of reportable items, the value for EEI filing shall be the value of the goods in US dollars at the port, airport or land border of export (or the cost if not sold). See 15CFR Part 30.6(a)(17). Estimates are permitted.

d. Import Entry Documentation: This is a buyer obligation. However, A7 requires the seller to provide assistance at the buyer's request, risk and cost.

8 Payment terms considerations

These transactions are frequently quite large. By definition, the seller must arrange for delivery next to the vessel. It then follows that the seller must be prepared to turn the goods over at that place. This means there's no way to use documents to restrict possession of the goods. This argues strongly for open account or payment in advance. It is possible that a mate's receipt or a sufficiently detailed dock receipt could be used to trigger a letter of credit. It is also possible that a sufficiently detailed negotiable freight collect received-for-shipment transportation document could be used both for letters of credit and documentary collections. However, as the seller is not contracting for main carriage, the risk exists that the buyer-appointed carrier or forwarder may not follow any seller-provided instructions, or may refuse to provide the needed document to the seller.

STORY LINE

None of the following examples involves the usual suspects.

The Furna Hotel and resort is located on the island of Brava, Cape Verde Islands. This area has lately become a popular tourist haven. Its port is too shallow to accommodate most vessels, so shipments are handled by a barge traveling between the port and visiting geared ships at anchor. The hotel's standby generator shorted out while under warranty, and the manufacturer sent a replacement. (See the DPU chapter for how it got there.) Warranty conditions included return of the defective unit. The hotel arranged its return on the same vessel that brought the replacement. Proforma FAS 1 illustrates shore to vessel lighterage.

The MV Tom Jordan is a Great Lakes boat[34] plying the iron ore route from Minnesota to Cleveland. The air conditioner compressor for the captain's stateroom failed during a heat wave in mid-August, and stopping for a minor repair would be cost prohibitive. A Detroit marine chandlery had a replacement on hand, and brought it to the J. W. Westcott Company for delivery with its shore-to-ship lighterage service. Proforma FAS 2.

In early 1979 then-prosperous Venezuela faced a major electrical generation emergency. An old major substation scheduled for replacement failed prematurely. The new replacement equipment on order was over a year away, backup equipment was stretched to the limit, and a major blackout of Caracas was likely unless substitute generation equipment could be put on line within weeks. Fortunately, the Puerto Rico Power Authority had two skid-mounted jet powered 10KW generators which had recently become surplus. However, they were located in remote rural communities and overland movement to a major port was impossible. The nearest port, Yabucoa, lacked heavy lift equipment. The Venezuelan Navy obligingly dispatched a shallow draft geared vessel which transported the generators in time to avoid a serious outage. Proforma FAS 3. Note: This took place long before Venezuela's current political and economic problems.

[34] Although huge, Great Lakes vessels are called boats.

AMERICAN VIEWPOINT

Quite a bit of cargo moves by chartered vessel in terms of tonnage. Bulk commodities are usually transported this way, although container imbalances have made U.S. produce exporters aware of the benefits of containerization. Huge pieces of project cargo are transported on geared vessels These shipments require detailed planning and execution by all parties.

International use

The Incoterms® rule tasks the seller with export clearance. This can be at odds with local regulations.

Routed transactions[35]: For U.S. exports, the Census Bureau's Foreign Trade Regulations require the party appointed by the buyer to handle export to file the Electronic Export Information (EEI). This usually translates to a buyer-appointed forwarder (or carrier as their roles are increasingly becoming interchangeable) . The seller, known as the United States Principal Party in Interest (USPPI), is required to provide this party with its company and product specific information needed to file the EEI. In return, the USPPI is entitled only to written confirmation from this service provider of the information it provided. The USPPI has no right to the transportation information in this situation as the EEI is confidential between the filer and Census.

As mentioned earlier and explained in more detail in the American Perspective chapter 24 there is relief for exporters that prefer to file their EEIs in routed transactions rather than trusting service providers over which they have no control. An additional payoff is access to the transportation information. Savvy sellers use this to help their forwarders obtain lower freight costs and better service in order to gain control of future shipments.

There are a few other potential seller risks with all F-Group rules that stem from the buyer's contracting for main carriage with the carrier. This normally means that the buyer also appoints the forwarder. Both of these service providers would therefore follow instructions from the buyer rather than any they may receive from the seller. This opens the possibility of diversion which could be illegal shipment to a prohibited party or country. More likely would be commercial diversion to a non-restricted party or country other than the destination desired by the seller. Depending on the product, doing so may or may not violate export regulations but in any event could seriously compromise the seller's distribution arrangements. Also, questionable seller access to transportation documents could present a problem with document-driven payment terms.

Speaking of payment terms, don't be surprised to receive letters of credit calling for freight collect "on board ocean bills of lading," extending the beneficiary's risk through vessel loading. Many banks simply will not accept a dock receipt or other "received for shipment" document, regardless of the fact that this agrees with the seller's FAS Incoterms® obligation. Others confuse the "on board-ness" with consignment instructions. (It is perfectly possible to have a negotiable received for shipment marine transportation document.) Unfortunately, as the buyer is contracting for main carriage, the seller who is beneficiary of such a letter of credit would be at payment risk for the loading operations of a carrier it did not choose and may never have chosen.

For chartering, the fact that the buyer selects the main carrier may not be so important for purely volume considerations. Charter shipments are often negotiated individually, largely depending on vessel availability for the desired ports and times.

Experienced U.S. importers can do well with FAS. U.S. import duty is not payable on freight to get here, so the FAS price is usually the dutiable value. Also, controlling the overseas forwarder really helps compliance, especially for shipments covered by the Importer Security Filing "10+2" reporting requirements.

---

[35] As of this writing, Census is working on possible revisions to the routed transaction rules.

Domestic use

FAS presents no problem for purely domestic transactions. Barge movements come to mind, and there is growing interest in "short-sea" shipments from one U.S. port to another.

PROFORMA INVOICE

EXPORTER Furna Hotel & Resort Pominade Brava Cape Verde Islands	**PROFORMA INVOICE #** FAS 1 **PROFORMA INVOICE DATE** September 30, 2020 **PROFORMA VALIDITY DATE** October 1, 2020 **EST'D SHIPMENT DATE** Tomorrow
SOLD TO Zap Electrics Ltd. 7 Queen Victoria Parade Belfast NO72OK United Kingdom	**TERMS OF PAYMENT** No Charge - Return of defective generator **SHIPMENT/DELIVERY TERMS** FAS Vessel Hesperus, Incoterms 2020
SHIP TO Shipside, offshore at Port Brava entrance	**TITLE** Warranty return

QUANTITY	UNITS	DESCRIPTION OF MERCHANDISE	UNIT PRICE	TOTAL
1	Each	Broken standby generator returned under warranty. Value for customs purposes original price of Lstg. 8,780.00	No charge	0.00

LAW & DISPUTE RESOLUTION: The U.N. Convention on Contracts for the International Sale of Goods (1980) shall apply to this offer and any resulting contract. Any disputes will be resolved by binding arbitration services of the International Chamber of Commerce.	**MERCHANDISE TOTAL**	0.00
	GRAND TOTAL FAS Hesperus, Brava, Cape Verde Is.	0.00

PROFORMA INVOICE

EXPORTER Detroit Chandlery Inc. 7 James Hoffa Street Detroit 48201 MI USA	**PROFORMA INVOICE #** FAS 2	**PROFORMA INVOICE DATE** September 30, 2020
	PROFORMA VALIDITY DATE October 1, 2020	**EST'D SHIPMENT DATE** Tomorrow
SOLD TO Akers Great Lakes Lines 5522 Dorr Street Toledo, OH 43615 USA	**TERMS OF PAYMENT** Net 30	
	SHIPMENT/DELIVERY TERMS FAS MV Tom Jordan, Presque Isle Cut, Lake Erie, Incoterms 2020	
SHIP TO Shipside, MV Tom Jordan, offshore at Presque Island Cut. (Boat to arrive October 1 at approximately 1300 hrs.)	**TITLE** Ownership passes at delivery	

QUANTITY	UNITS	DESCRIPTION OF MERCHANDISE	UNIT PRICE	TOTAL
1	Each	Air conditioner compressor for CoolAire model 302 Package weight 83 lbs., dimensions 27" x 30" x9"	$ 875.00	$875.00

LAW & DISPUTE RESOLUTION: The law of the state of Michigan shall apply to this offer and any resulting contract. Any disputes will be resolved by binding arbitration services of the American Arbitration Association.	**MERCHANDISE TOTAL** **Freight** (delivery ship-ship by Wescott Co. tender)	$875.00 $385.00
	GRAND TOTAL FAS MV Tom Jordan	$1,260.00

PROFORMA INVOICE

EXPORTER PRWRA San Juan, Puerto Rico	**PROFORMA INVOICE #** FAS 3 **PROFORMA INVOICE DATE** April 1, 1979 **PROFORMA VALIDITY DATE** May 1, 1979 **EST'D SHIPMENT DATE** June 15, 1979
SOLD TO Venezuela Fuerza (VF) Avenida 1 Simon Bolivar, Oficina 204 Caracas, Venezuela	**TERMS OF PAYMENT** Irrevocable letter of credit with payment against clean dock receipt **SHIPMENT/DELIVERY TERMS** FAS Quay Puerto Yabucoa, Puerto Rico, Incoterms 1974
SHIP TO Quay, Puerto Yabucoa, Puerto Rico	**TITLE** Ownership passes when payment is received by seller

QUANTITY	UNITS	DESCRIPTION OF MERCHANDISE	UNIT PRICE	TOTAL
2	Each	Used, Powermaster skid mounted 10 MW jet powered generators, inspected at site by VF engineers on March 17, 1979, sold AS IS.	US$ 7,200,000.00	US$14,400,000.00

LAW & DISPUTE RESOLUTION: The Commercial Code of the Estado Asociado Libre de Puerto Rico (Associated Free State of Puerto Rico).	**MERCHANDISE TOTAL EXW** **Pre-carriage to Yabucoa** **Crating**	$14,400,000.00 $27,500.00 $8,300.00
	GRAND TOTAL FAS Yabucoa, PR	$14,435,800.00

CHAPTER 14 - FREE ON BOARD

Abbreviation: FOB
Transport mode: vessel only
Contract type: shipment
Place: loaded onto a buyer-appointed vessel at the agreed port on the seller's side

Free On Board (FOB) is probably the oldest shipment-delivery term, predating not only Incoterms®[36] rules but ship lines. It is widely overused, particularly in the United States. Its correct Incoterms® use should be limited to non-containerized waterborne shipments where the buyer contracts for main carriage and the seller handles vessel loading.

A4 of the FOB rule states that the seller is not tasked with providing carriage. However, the accompanying place is on board a buyer-appointed vessel, and the seller must get the goods there in order to deliver. The "no obligation for carriage" refers to main carriage.

The concept of "ship's rail" was dropped from the FOB rule in Incoterms® 2010. Sellers deliver the goods when they are on board the buyer-appointed vessel. This is not as significant as it first appears, as the "Contract of Carriage" task lines in both *Incoterms® 2000*[37]® and *Incoterms® 2010*[38] both said "on board." However, removal of the "ship's rail" phrase could increase seller responsibility. As "on board" is not defined, the parties should agree on exactly what this entails, particularly for charter movements. This can vary, depending on the type of cargo and vessel.

A2 of the FOB rule also retains the 2010 provision covering goods that have already been delivered. This is intended to facilitate the use of this rule in commodity trade, where goods are commonly sold while in transit (so called "string sales").

FOB reflects the way most cargo was handled prior to containerization. Ports were little more than collections of piers to which outbound cargo was delivered. Nowadays, most modern container ports are very secure areas. Outbound containerized cargo is normally handed over some distance from the ships. Further, most scheduled ship lines load and unload their own vessels which they can do as they regularly call on the same ports. Still, there are instances where FOB is appropriate:

- with vessel chartering under "free in" terms, where the seller handles vessel loading while the buyer handles main carriage, as is common in commodity trades or with break-bulk shipments of project cargo,
- other marine transport situations where the seller is better positioned to load,
- when the seller is willing to remain responsible for the terminal handling charges and loading charges and the loading performance of a buyer-appointed carrier,
- when the goods are sold after they have been loaded,
- with containers at small or less developed ports,
- where there is uncertainty about the seller's ability to timely deliver the goods.

Despite the fact that its correct use is limited, and that FCA + on board could be a substitute, it is unlikely that the FOB Incoterms® rule will be discarded for many years to come. There are simply too many legacy issues.

The FOB rule is used for shipment contracts as the seller delivers when the goods are loaded on the buyer-appointed vessel at the agreed place at the agreed port within the agreed time frame.

---

[36] Incoterms® is a trademark of the International Chamber of Commerce, registered in several countries.

[37] *Incoterms® 2000*, ICC Publishing SA, Paris, France, ICC Publication no. 560, ISBN 92-842-1199-9

[38] *Incoterms® 2010*, ICC Publishing SA, Paris, France, ICC Publication no. 715E, ISBN 978 -92-842-0080-1

The seller must also notify the buyer either that the goods have been delivered or that the buyer-appointed carrier has failed to receive them.

The location within the port should be described in geographic terms in as much detail as possible. With charter vessels, timing is extremely important because of the costs of needlessly tying up an entire vessel. Conversely, there are significant costs and risks in having goods arrive prematurely at a port awaiting the vessel. Sellers, buyers and carriers should work closely to coordinate the ship's arrival and the delivery of the goods.

Sellers are responsible for export clearance under this Incoterms® rule. Exporters need to exercise due diligence as they are not in a position to know the disposition of their shipments once they are delivered. However, as they are putting the goods on a buyer-appointed vessel, they are a transport leg closer to the actual export than is the case with EXW or FCA + seller's premises. Savvy U.S. exporters use the Census Bureau's FTRs to their advantage by obtaining written authorizations from their buyers to file the EEIs. They then insist that the buyer-appointed forwarders and carriers[39] provide the transportation information pre-shipment in writing to enable them to file. The buyers should have no reluctance to provide authorizations since under the FOB rule they have already agreed that the sellers handle export clearance. In fact, any buyer reluctance should be treated with suspicion as it would be contrary to the terms of the sales contract.

Note: Although contracting for any main carriage is strictly speaking a buyer obligation; sellers sometimes take on this task for the buyers at the buyers' risk and cost. The resulting documentation would be a freight-prepaid transport document, with carriage arrangements made by the seller for the account of the buyer. Using some circular logic, this can be said to work to the seller's advantage. By contracting for main carriage, the seller selects the carrier and presumably could claim in case of damage during the loading process. The question remains, why the seller wouldn't then opt for CFR or CIF rather than a convoluted FOB. (I did mention circular logic.)

BUYER-SELLER RESPONSIBILITIES

The following is a short list of responsibilities.

1. **Goods and Payment**
   The seller must have the goods available when promised, suitably packaged, and must transport them and load them onto the agreed vessel at the agreed port on the seller's side. The buyer must pay the seller.
2. **Loading and unloading**
   The seller is responsible for loading the goods onto the buyer appointed vessel.
3. **Pre-carriage**
   This is a seller responsibility under this rule.
4. **Export clearance**
   This is a seller responsibility under this rule.
5. **Other hoops and hurdles**
   The parties must work together on cargo security information. This usually means one party telling the other what is required and the other party providing it. Since security regulations change often and vary from country to country and from one transport mode to another, Incoterms® rules are limited to making the parties aware that they must be addressed. This is covered in A4-B4 and A7-B7.

[39] The roles of carrier and forwarder have largely merged in today's transportation practice, with chartering as a possible exception.

6. **Insurance**

Neither party is required to insure under FOB. However, common sense dictates otherwise, and insurance should be addressed outside of the rule. Sellers are at risk until the goods are placed on board the vessel. (Check with your insurers about FAS/FOB coverage). Buyers are at risk thereafter.

7. **Documentary implications**
   a. Commercial Documents: The seller should provide a commercial invoice, a packing list, and any other commercial documents cited in the sales contract.
   b. Transport Documents: The seller should provide evidence that the contract goods were loaded on the vessel. This should be an "on board" freight collect marine transport document.
   c. Export Control Documentation: The seller is obligated to handle export clearance under this Incoterms® rule. In a routed transaction, as the USPPI the seller is obligated at a minimum to provide company and product specific information to the buyer-appointed agent for EEI filing. Proactive sellers who obtain buyer authorizations and file the EEIs will have an electronic record of filing. Note: for U.S. exports of reportable items, the value for EEI filing shall be the value of the goods in US dollars at the port, airport or land border of export (or the cost if not sold). See 15CFR Part 30.6(a)(17). Estimates are permitted.
   d. Import Entry Documentation: This is a buyer obligation. However, A7 requires the seller to provide assistance at the buyer's request, risk and cost.

8. **Payment terms considerations**

By definition, the seller must arrange for loading the goods onto the vessel. The only appropriate document would be one indicating that the goods are "on board." Since the buyer is contracting for transportation, it would be freight collect. This document could be used to trigger a letter of credit. If negotiable (consigned to "order") it can also be used for documentary collections. However, as the seller is not contracting for main carriage, the risk exists that the buyer-appointed carrier or forwarder may not follow any seller-provided instructions, or may refuse to provide the needed document to the seller.

STORY LINE

None of the "usual suspects" would dream of using the FOB Incoterms® rule in day-to-day business. However, Glotz had some very large surplus equipment that was in good condition. It couldn't achieve the production economies needed for North America, but could be perfectly useful in a smaller market with lower labor costs. A Vietnamese manufacturer heard about it through a machinery broker and determined that it would suit his fledging operation. Glotz quoted an FAS price that included disassembling the equipment and transporting it to a Great Lakes port where they were able to obtain permission to bring it pier side. The buyer chartered space on a small tramp vessel that called on that port. However, the intended vessel was damaged en-route, and the last minute replacement did not have a large enough crane. As a concession to the buyer, Glotz bravely agreed to handle vessel loading for an additional $6,709.00 to cover loading charges as shown in proforma invoice FOB-1. The parties agreed to have the letter of credit amended to require a clean on board freight collect bill of lading rather than the clean dock receipt indicating shipside delivery that was originally required.

AMERICAN VIEWPOINT

Quite a bit of cargo moves by chartered vessel in terms of tonnage. Bulk commodities are usually transported this way (although container imbalances have made U.S. produce exporters aware of the benefits of containerization). Huge pieces of project cargo too large for containers are shipped this way. These shipments require detailed planning and execution by all parties. FOB works particularly well for products typically loaded by sellers from pier-side facilities, such as liquids from tank farms, grain from elevators, etc.

International use
While this Incoterms® rule tasks the seller with export clearance, this can be at odds with local regulations.

Routed transactions[40]: For U.S. exports, the Census Bureau's Foreign Trade Regulations require the party appointed by the buyer to handle export to file the Electronic Export Information (EEI). This usually translates to a buyer-appointed forwarder (or carrier as their roles are increasingly becoming interchangeable). The seller, known as the United States Principal Party in Interest (USPPI), is required to provide this party with its company and product specific information needed to file the EEI. In return, the USPPI is entitled only to written confirmation from this service provider of the information it provided. The USPPI has no right to the transportation information in this situation as the EEI is confidential between the filer and Census.

As mentioned earlier and explained in more detail in the American Perspective chapter 24, there is relief for exporters that prefer to file their EEIs in routed transactions rather than trusting service providers over which they have no control. An additional payoff is access to the transportation information. Savvy sellers use this to help their forwarders obtain lower freight costs and better service in order to gain control of future shipments.

There are a few other potential seller risks with all F-Group rules that stem from the buyer's contracting for main carriage with the carrier. This normally means that the buyer also appoints the forwarder. Both of these service providers would therefore follow instructions from the buyer rather than any they receive from the seller. This opens the possibility of diversion which could be illegal shipment to a prohibited party or country. More likely would be commercial diversion to a non-restricted party or country other than the destination desired by the seller. Depending on the product, doing so may or may not violate export regulations but in any event could seriously compromise the seller's distribution arrangements. Also, lack of assured access to transportation documents could present a problem for sellers, particularly with document-driven payment terms.

Banks are quite attached to "on board ocean bills of lading." The writer discussed this with a letter of credit expert friend who also has a good command of the way transactions really work. He provided an example of how important it can be for goods to be actually vessel loaded with time-imperative goods: fresh cut Christmas trees! Granted, but most shipments aren't so time-imperative. Part of the problem is that both FOB and letters of credit predate containerized transportation. The "thus it has always been and thus it shall remain" mindset completely ignores the fact that in most cases sellers hand over the contract goods to buyer-appointed carriers some distance from vessels. Incoterms® 2020 rules attempt to address this problem by bringing the issue of on-board documentation into the FCA rule.

For chartering, the fact that the buyer selects the main carrier may not be so important for purely volume considerations. Charter shipments are often negotiated individually, largely depending on vessel availability for the desired ports and times. However, for non-charter movements VOLUME is king, and sellers seeking large shipper status are not helped by shipments on F-Group rules.

Experienced U.S. importers can do well with FOB. U.S. import duty is not payable on freight to get here, so the FOB price is usually the dutiable value. Also, controlling the overseas forwarder really helps compliance, especially for containerized, break-bulk or Ro-Ro[41] shipments covered by the Importer Security Filing (10+2) reporting requirements.

In the past, some trade associations complained of complicity between carriers and buyers with the use of the FOB rule with containerized shipments. Buyers received low pure freight costs, while sellers were billed exaggerated terminal handling charges.

---

[40] As of this writing, Census is working on possible revisions to the routed transaction rules.

[41] Roll-on, roll-off, where cargo is either driven on board as with car carriers or mounted on small dedicated trailers which are towed on board.

Domestic use

Used correctly the FOB Incoterms® 2020 rule presents no problem for purely domestic transactions. Barge movements come to mind, and there is growing interest in "short-sea" shipments from one U.S. port to another.

A Final Word on FOB

The old "FOB here, there and everywhere" shipment and delivery term remains in the Uniform Commercial Code and in general domestic use. It is possible that farsighted U.S. buyers and sellers will continue using Incoterms® 2020 rules in domestic trade for convenience reasons. Readers will find a match-up from the old UCC shipment and delivery terms to Incoterms® 2010 rules in the last chapter of this book.

PROFORMA INVOICE

EXPORTER Glotz Industries Inc 1492 Columbus Boulevard Fort Wayne, Indiana 12345-6789 USA	**PROFORMA INVOICE #** FOB 1 **PROFORMA INVOICE DATE** December 1, 2020 **PROFORMA VALIDITY DATE** December 31, 2020 **EST'D SHIPMENT DATE** December 15, 2020
SOLD TO Vietnam Widgets Ltd. 4 Nixon Way Ho Chi Minh City VIETNAM	**TERMS OF PAYMENT** Irrevocable, confirmed letter of credit, payable at sight **SHIPMENT/DELIVERY TERMS** FOB Port of Toledo, Ohio, USA, Incoterms 2020
SHIP TO Port of Toledo Toledo, Ohio USA	**TITLE** Ownership transfers when payment is received by seller

QUANTITY	UNITS	DESCRIPTION OF MERCHANDISE	UNIT PRICE	TOTAL
1	Each	Used, complete widget manufacturing machine serial # 718-56, tested and operating at seller's premises before disassembly and shipment	973,500.00	973,500.00

LAW & DISPUTE RESOLUTION: The U.N. Convention on Contracts for the International Sale of Goods (1980) shall apply to this offer and any resulting contract. Any disputes will be resolved by binding arbitration services of the International Chamber of Commerce.	**MERCHANDISE TOTAL** Export Packing Pre carriage to port Terminal handling Heavy lift & loading	**US$** 973500.00 7230.00 3192.00 625.00 6709.00
	GRAND TOTAL FOB Toledo Port, Ohio	**US$** 991,256.00

CHAPTER 15 - C-GROUP RULES

There are four C-Group rules: CPT, CIP, CFR and CIF. CPT and CIP were designed for use with all transport modes while CFR and CIF should be used only when main carriage is done by vessel.

The main thing that C-Group rules have in common is that the seller is responsible for main carriage. This means the seller selects and contracts with the main carrier. It usually means that the seller also selects the freight forwarder as the roles of carrier and forwarder have blended to the point where they are almost indistinguishable.

All C-Group rules are used in shipment contracts. Sellers deliver by handing over the contract goods to carriers somewhere on the seller's side, despite the fact that they contract for main carriage to the buyer's side.

SELLERS

C-Group rules are by far the most advantageous for sellers. As sellers contract for main carriage, they are in a position to give meaningful instructions to the carriers and forwarders they appoint. This provides a comfort level with document-driven payment terms and export compliance. Despite the fact that the seller contracts for carriage, its risk for the condition of the contract goods ends somewhere prior to main carriage. Sellers that frequently select carriers are in a position to negotiate favorable freight rates, thereby reducing the total cost to their customers or even creating freight-cost profit centers. Export reporting is a seller obligation, consistent with both "standard transactions" under the Census' Foreign Trade Regulations and with the Incoterms®[42] rule.

The only downsides for sellers are that there is more work involved than with F-Group rules. Contracting for carriage also provides a greater possibility for inexperienced sellers to make mistakes. Finally, sellers need to obtain and offer extremely competitive freight costs to make C-Group rules acceptable to experienced buyers.

BUYERS

Experienced buyers are usually not well served by C-Group rules unless their suppliers obtain exceptionally low freight costs. (Even then, a case can be made for D-Group rules.) The risk of being responsible for the condition of the contract goods while in transit with a carrier selected and paid by someone else should be considered. (Two C-Group rules CIP and CIF, help with this by requiring sellers to provide insurance cover.) U.S. importers must rely heavily on their suppliers for information on shipments subject to Importer Security Filing (ISF) pre-shipment reporting requirements.

HINT

CPT + Insurance = CIP, CFR + insurance = CIF

---

[42] Incoterms® is a trademark of the International Chamber of Commerce, registered in several countries.

CHAPTER 16 - CARRIAGE PAID TO

Abbreviation: CPT
Transport mode: all
Contract type: shipment
Place: somewhere on the buyer's side of transportation

Carriage Paid To (CPT) and its first cousin, Carriage and Insurance Paid (CIP) are the most versatile of the C-Group Incoterms® rules. The difference between the two is that under CPT, no one is required to insure (although the buyer should have strong commercial interest in doing so outside the Incoterm® rule). Both rules can be used with any mode of transportation. The place must be on the buyer's side of transportation for which the seller contracts. For international trade, possibilities include an arrival point (port, airport, etc.) or anywhere else on the buyer's side that the parties agree, including the buyer's premises. For domestic trade, it's at the end of transportation contracted for by the seller and agreed by the parties. Whatever place the parties select should be spelled out in as much detail as possible, including street addresses when available.

Sellers should carefully contract for transportation to match the agreed point at the agreed place, since buyers are not required to reimburse them for any additional costs beyond that point. This omnimodal rule is so versatile that no destination place can be set as a default. For instance, with vessel shipments, unloading can involve terminal handling and other such costs which do not apply to other transport modes like small package carriers. Since there is no consistency as to how and to whom carriers levy these charges, the parties should address this in their sales contract and sellers should contract for transportation accordingly.

CPT may be used with single carrier or multimodal transportation.

For international trade, CPT works particularly well when the seller contracts for door-to-agreed-place-on-buyer's-side (also called "through") carriage. The reason is that the default delivery position for this rule is that the seller delivers by handing over the contract goods to the FIRST carrier.

When the first carrier is part of a carriage contract written on a door-to-agreed-place-on-the-buyer's-side basis, the buyer should be able to claim on the main carrier even for mishaps that occur in pre-carriage. By contrast, let's suppose there are separate contracts for pre-carriage and main carriage. If there is loss or damage to the goods in pre-carriage, the foreign buyer is left in the unenviable position of trying to claim on the pre-carrier located in the seller's country. The seller is out of the picture as far as delivery is concerned as its risk ended with handing over the contract goods to the pre-carrier. However, it can be argued that since the problem occurred prior to main carriage, the seller failed in its obligation to contract for transportation to the named destination shown in A4.

Ending the seller's risk at the first carrier may seem odd at first as under CPT the seller selects and contracts with the carrier. However, it is consistent with Article 67 of the United Nations Convention Contracts for the International Sale of Goods (CISG). Also, the first carrier provision was specified ever since the CPT rule was created in *Incoterms 1990*[43]. Realizing that the risk transfer point may not be obvious to persons not already familiar with Incoterms® use, *Incoterms®*[44] *2020*[45] goes out of its way to call attention to this situation

---

[43] *Incoterms 1990*, ICC Publishing SA, Paris, France, ICC Publication no. 460, ISBN 92-842-0087-3

[44] Incoterms® is a trademark of the International Chamber of Commerce, registered in several countries.

[45] *Incoterms® 2020*, ICC Publishing SA, Paris, France, ICC Publication no. 723E, ISBN 978-92-842-0510-3

both in the Explanatory Notes for this rule and in the Introduction. Parties in their sales contracts may agree that delivery happens in a different place than at the first carrier, such as when and where the goods are handed over to a main carrier. They may also agree to use a different Incoterms® rule altogether, such as DAP.

The same risk is of course present in domestic use. However, much of our domestic transportation is done on a door-to-door basis, and this default situation would occur only when more than one contract of carriage is involved. Also, both the domestic buyer and the pre-carrier are in this country.

International shipments are accommodated since sellers are responsible for export clearance. This is consistent with "standard transactions" under Census' Foreign Trade Regulations.

Since the seller is contracting for carriage, it usually also appoints the forwarder for international transactions. This enables the seller to provide instructions to these parties without the risk of their following any conflicting instructions from the buyer.

A4 of the CPT rule includes a provision covering procurement of a contract covering goods that have already been shipped. This is intended to facilitate the use of this rule in commodity trade, where goods are commonly sold while in transit (so called "string sales").

BUYER-SELLER RESPONSIBILITIES

The following is a short list of responsibilities.

1. **Goods and Payment**
   The seller must ship the goods when promised, and must promptly notify the buyer that they have done so. The buyer must pay the seller.
   Since the seller is arranging transport, it should be aware of what packaging is needed.
2. **Loading and unloading**
   The seller is responsible for loading the collecting conveyance, and the buyer is responsible for unloading the delivering conveyance.
3. **Pre-carriage and main carriage (and on-carriage?)**
   The seller is responsible for payment of carriage to the agreed place. However, the default position is that the seller delivers by handing over the goods to the first carrier, which could cause problems unless carriage is contracted on a "door-to-agreed-place-on-buyer's-side" ("through") basis.
4. **Export clearance**
   This is a seller responsibility under this rule.
5. **Other hoops and hurdles**
   The parties must work together on cargo security information. This usually means one party telling the other what is required and the other party providing it. Since security regulations change often and vary from country to country and from one transport mode to another, Incoterms® rules are limited to making the parties aware that they must be addressed. This is covered in A4-B4 and A7-B7.
6. **Insurance**
   Neither party is required to insure under CPT. However, common sense dictates otherwise, and the buyer should consider insurance outside of the rule.
7. **Documentary implications**
   a. Commercial Documents: The seller should provide a commercial invoice, a packing list, and any other commercial documents cited in the sales contract.
   b. Transport Documents: The seller must provide a freight-prepaid transport document to the agreed place if requested by the buyer.

c. Export Control Documentation: The seller is obligated to handle export clearance under this Incoterms® rule. Since the seller usually selects the freight forwarder, it is also obligated to handle export reporting under the Census Foreign Trade Regulations. Note: for U.S. exports of reportable items, the value for EEI filing shall be the value of the goods in US dollars at the port, airport or land border of export (or the cost if not sold). See 15CFR Part 30.6(a)(17). Estimates are permitted.
d. Import Entry Documentation: This is a buyer obligation. However, A7 requires the seller to provide assistance at the buyer's request, risk and cost.

8. **Payment terms considerations**
By definition, the seller must arrange and pay for carriage to the agreed place. This means the seller is in a position to require the forwarder and carrier to provide transport documentation to its specifications, and will have access to them for use in both for letters of credit and documentary collections.

STORY LINE

Otto and Andre

Otto is a young importer of widgets located in Baden Baden, Germany. Andre is Otto's French widget supplier, located in Strasbourg, France, quite near the German border. Although Otto has negotiated very good freight rates with a truck line serving Strassburg and Baden-Baden, Andre has an even better rate with a small package carrier which they use for very small shipments and next-day service. See proforma CPT 1.

Otto and Glotz

Otto wishes to purchase from Glotz Industries, a Fort Wayne widget manufacturer. Both are literally starting from scratch. After Otto rejected Glotz's EXW proposal, Glotz requoted using the FCA Incoterms® rule. Otto requested another quotation on a freight-paid basis for comparison, and Glotz quoted CPT. See proforma CPT 2.

Gordie and Glotz

Occasionally, Glotz can obtain a "sweetheart" freight rate that beats anything Gordie can come up with. Because of cabotage agreements between the U.S. and Canada, the same truck line that picks up at Glotz's factory delivers at Gordie's warehouse. See Glotz's proforma invoice CPT 3.

Riddle and Glotz

Riddle always gets lower freight costs, and never purchases on a freight-prepaid basis.

AMERICAN VIEWPOINT

International use

This Incoterms® rule tasks the seller with export clearance. For US exporters, this is consistent with the "standard transaction" definition of Foreign Trade Regulations. The seller, known as the United States Principal Party in Interest (USPPI), is required to file the EEI or appoint an agent to do so, usually a seller-appointed forwarder. As the USPPI is contracting for transportation, it will have the necessary transportation information to file.

Delivery at the first carrier can cause problems for inexperienced users when pre-carriage is contracted independently of main carriage. Here's an extreme example. A "mom & pop" truck line was transporting an expensive yacht to a seaport for shipment against a port-to-port contract of main carriage. The truck crashed on the Indiana Toll Road and never reached the port. Sadly, mom, pop, the truck and the yacht are no more. As the seller has already delivered, upon whom does the foreign buyer claim? One answer would be the seller, for failing to contract for main carriage because the yacht never arrived at the main carrier's terminal.

As through transportation is impossible in this situation, a far better solution for this situation would be for the parties to agree outside the Incoterm® rule that delivery take place at the main carrier's terminal on the seller's side.

Since both the carrier and presumably the forwarder are working for the seller, there should be no problem obtaining documents necessary to make payment terms work. However, don't be surprised to receive letters of credit calling for "on board freight prepaid ocean bills of lading," extending the beneficiary's risk through vessel loading and resulting in a CFR-like situation. Many banks simply will not accept a "received for shipment" document, regardless of the fact that this agrees with the seller's CPT Incoterms® obligation. Others confuse the "on board-ness" with consignment instructions. It is perfectly possible to have a negotiable received for shipment freight prepaid marine transportation document. Fortunately, as the seller is contracting for main carriage, it is not terribly unreasonable that it be responsible for the carrier's main carriage loading obligations.

Another seller advantage is that each shipment made under C-Group Incoterms® rules is that is counted to its credit in negotiating shippers' agreements. Since the seller is the party contracting for transportation with the carrier, it is the shipper. Service providers respect VOLUME above all. Shippers that control many shipments have, do, and always will pay lower freight costs and get better service than less frequent shippers.

Experienced U.S. importers may prefer to buy on an F-Group term unless their suppliers offer exceptionally attractive freight costs. Even where this is the case, consider holding the seller responsible for the carrier it chooses by requesting DPU or DAP rather than C-Group rules. These rules also take the "first carrier" situation off the table by equating delivery with arrival. In any case, insist on proof of what the freight costs are (such as a rated transport document) to avoid paying import duty on inbound freight costs.

Domestic use
Except for buyers attempting to achieve large shipper status, CPT presents no problem for purely domestic transactions.

PROFORMA INVOICE

<table>
<tr><td rowspan="2">EXPORTER
Les Widgets de France
Rue John-Pierre Robin 12
Strasbourg
FRANCE</td><td>PROFORMA INVOICE #
CPT 1</td><td>PROFORMA INVOICE DATE
October 2, 2020</td></tr>
<tr><td>PROFORMA VALIDITY DATE
November 2, 2020</td><td>EST'D SHIPMENT DATE
October 6, 2020</td></tr>
<tr><td rowspan="2">SOLD TO
Widgets by Otto III
Dean Haberkampstrasse
Baden Baden
GERMANY</td><td colspan="2">TERMS OF PAYMENT
Net 30 days</td></tr>
<tr><td colspan="2">SHIPMENT/DELIVERY TERMS
CPT Dean Haberkampstrasse, Baden Baden, Germany, Incoterms 2020</td></tr>
<tr><td>SHIP TO
Same as SOLD TO</td><td colspan="2">TITLE
Ownership transfers when payment is received by seller</td></tr>
</table>

QUANTITY	UNITS	DESCRIPTION OF MERCHANDISE	UNIT PRICE	TOTAL
40	Each	Bleu widgets	€ 100.00	€ 4000.00

<table>
<tr><td rowspan="2">LAW & DISPUTE RESOLUTION: The U.N. Convention on Contracts for the International Sale of Goods (1980) shall apply to this offer and any resulting contract. Any disputes will be resolved by binding arbitration services of the International Chamber of Commerce.</td><td>MERCHANDISE TOTAL
Freight</td><td>€ 4000.00
809.00</td></tr>
<tr><td>GRAND TOTAL
CPT Baden Baden</td><td>€ 4809.00</td></tr>
</table>

PROFORMA INVOICE

EXPORTER Glotz Industries Inc 1492 Columbus Boulevard Fort Wayne, Indiana 12345-6789 USA	**PROFORMA INVOICE #** CPT 2 **PROFORMA INVOICE DATE** October 15, 2020 **PROFORMA VALIDITY DATE** November 15, 2020 **EST'D SHIPMENT DATE** November 1, 2020
SOLD TO Widgets by Otto III Dean Haberkampstrasse Baden Baden GERMANY	**TERMS OF PAYMENT** Net 30 days **SHIPMENT/DELIVERY TERMS** CPT Air America Terminal, Frankfurt Airport, Frankfurt, Germany, Incoterms 2020
SHIP TO Air America Terminal, Frankfurt Airport Frankfurt GERMANY	**TITLE** Ownership transfers when payment is received by seller

QUANTITY	UNITS	DESCRIPTION OF MERCHANDISE	UNIT PRICE	TOTAL
20	Each	Blue widgets	100.00	2000.00

LAW & DISPUTE RESOLUTION: The U.N. Convention on Contracts for the International Sale of Goods (1980) shall apply to this offer and any resulting contract. Any disputes will be resolved by binding arbitration services of the International Chamber of Commerce.	**MERCHANDISE TOTAL** Export Packing Pre carriage Air Freight Forwarding	**US$** 2000.00 123.00 138.00 521.00 100.00
	GRAND TOTAL CPT Frankfurt	**US$** 2882.00

PROFORMA INVOICE

EXPORTER Glotz Industries Inc 1492 Columbus Boulevard Fort Wayne, Indiana 12345-6789 USA	**PROFORMA INVOICE #** CPT 3 **PROFORMA INVOICE DATE** October 15, 2020 **PROFORMA VALIDITY DATE** November 15, 2020 **EST'D SHIPMENT DATE** October 19, 2020
SOLD TO Gordie's Good Widgets 1 Carl Crewson Street North Bay, Ontario CANADA	**TERMS OF PAYMENT** Net 30 days **SHIPMENT/DELIVERY TERMS** CPT 1 Carl Crewson Street, North Bay, Ontario, Canada, Incoterms 2020
SHIP TO Same as SOLD TO	**TITLE** Ownership transfers when payment is received by seller

QUANTITY	UNITS	DESCRIPTION OF MERCHANDISE	UNIT PRICE	TOTAL
40	Each	Blue widgets	100.00	4000.00

LAW & DISPUTE RESOLUTION: The U.N. Convention on Contracts for the International Sale of Goods (1980) shall apply to this offer and any resulting contract. Any disputes will be resolved by binding arbitration services of the International Chamber of Commerce.	**MERCHANDISE TOTAL** Freight	**US$** 4000.00 392.00
	GRAND TOTAL CPT North Bay	**US$** 4392.00

CHAPTER 17 - CARRIAGE AND INSURANCE PAID

Abbreviation: CIP
Transport mode: all
Contract type: shipment
Place: somewhere on the buyer's side of transportation

Carriage and Insurance Paid (CIP) and its first cousin, Carriage Paid To (CPT) are the most versatile of the C-Group Incoterms®[46] rules. The difference between the two is that under CIP the seller is required to insure. Both rules can be used with any mode of transportation. The place must be on the buyer's side of transportation for which the seller contracts. For international trade, possibilities include an arrival point (port, airport, etc.) or anywhere else on the buyer's side that the parties agree, including the buyer's premises. For domestic trade, it's at the end of transportation contracted for by the seller and agreed by the parties. Whatever place the parties select should be spelled out in as much detail as possible, including street addresses when available.

Sellers should carefully contract for transportation to match the agreed point at the agreed place, since buyers are not required to reimburse them for any additional costs beyond that point. This omnimodal rule is so versatile that no destination place can be set as a default. For instance, with vessel shipments, unloading can involve terminal handling and other such costs which do not apply to other transport modes like small package carriers. Since there is no consistency as to how and to whom carriers levy these charges, the parties should address this in their sales contract and sellers should contract for transportation accordingly.

CIP may be used with single carrier or multimodal transportation.

For international trade, CIP works particularly well when the seller contracts for door-to-agreed- place-on-buyer's-side (also called "through" carriage). The reason is that the default delivery position for this rule is that the seller delivers by handing over the contract goods to the FIRST carrier.

When the first carrier is part of a carriage contract written on a door-to-agreed-place-on-buyer's-side basis, the buyer should be able to claim on the main carrier even for mishaps that occur in pre-carriage.
By contrast, let's suppose there are separate contracts for pre-carriage and main carriage. If there is loss or damage to the goods in pre-carriage, the foreign buyer is left in the unenviable position of trying to claim on a pre-carrier located in the seller's country. The seller is out of the picture as far as delivery is concerned as its risk ended with handing over the contract goods to the pre-carrier. However, it can be argued that since the problem occurred prior to main carriage, the seller failed in its obligation to contract for transportation to the named destination shown in A4.

Another provision may come to the buyer's rescue under CIP. The seller is now obligated to provide insurance on an Institute Cargo Clauses A basis (so called "All Risk" in American) in such a way that the buyer may claim directly from the insurer. When this is provided on a warehouse to warehouse basis, the buyer should be able to claim on the insurer for any mishap in pre-carriage.

Ending the seller's risk at the first carrier may seem odd at first as under CIP the seller selects and contracts with the carrier. However, it is consistent with Article 67 of the United Nations Convention Contracts for the International Sale of Goods (CISG). Also, the first carrier provision was specified ever since

---

[46] Incoterms® is a trademark of the International Chamber of Commerce, registered in several countries.

the CIP rule was created in *Incoterms 1990*[47]. Realizing that the risk transfer point may not be obvious to persons not already familiar with Incoterms® use, *Incoterms® 2020*[48] goes out of its way to point this out in both the Explanatory Notes for this rule and in the Introduction. Parties in their sales contracts may agree that delivery happens in a different place than at the first carrier, such as when and where the goods are handed over to a main carrier. They may also agree to use a different Incoterms® rule altogether, such as DAP.

The same risk is of course present in domestic use. However, much of our domestic transportation is done on a door-to-door basis, and this default situation would occur only when more than one contract of carriage is involved. Also, both the domestic buyer and the pre-carrier are in this country.

International shipments are accommodated since sellers are responsible for export clearance. This is consistent with "standard transactions" under Census' Foreign Trade Regulations.

Since the seller is contracting for carriage, it usually also appoints the forwarder for international transactions. This enables the seller to provide instructions to these parties without the risk of their following any conflicting instructions from the buyer.

A4 of the CIP rule includes a provision covering procurement of a contract covering goods that have already been shipped. This is intended to facilitate the use of this rule in commodity trade, where goods are commonly sold while in transit (so called "string sales").

The CIP rule stipulates that the seller must provide insurance, and as mentioned earlier now requires Institute Cargo Clauses A (so called "All Risk" in American) coverage. This is new. Please note that this applies only to CIP and that the minimum insurance obligation for CIF remains minimum cover unless the parties agree otherwise. One reason for the difference is that goods sold under CIP are more likely to be high-value manufactured goods than is true with CIF.

Please refer to the Insurance chapter 8 of this book for further guidance.

BUYER-SELLER RESPONSIBILITIES

The following is a short list of responsibilities.

1. **Goods and Payment**
   The seller must ship the goods when promised, and must promptly notify the buyer that they have done so. The buyer must pay the seller.
   Since the seller is arranging transport, it should be aware of what packaging is needed.
2. **Loading and unloading**
   The seller is responsible for loading the collecting conveyance, and the buyer is responsible for unloading the delivering conveyance.

3. **Pre-carriage and main carriage (and on-carriage?)**
   The seller is responsible for payment of carriage to the agreed place. However, the default position is that the seller delivers by handing over the goods to the first carrier, which could cause problems unless carriage is contracted on a "door-to-agreed-place" ("through') basis.
4. **Export clearance**
   This is a seller responsibility under this rule.

---

[47] *Incoterms 1990*, ICC Publishing SA, Paris, France, ICC Publication no. 460, ISBN 92-842-0087-3

[48] *Incoterms® 2020*, ICC Publishing SA, Paris, France, ICC Publication no. 723E, ISBN 978-92-842-0510-3

5. **Other hoops and hurdles**
   The parties must work together on cargo security information. This usually means one party telling the other what is required and the other party providing it. Since security regulations change often and vary from country to country and from one transport mode to another, Incoterms® rules are limited to making the parties aware that they must be addressed. This is covered in A4-B4 and A7-B7.
6. **Insurance**
   The seller is required to provide Institute Cargo Clauses A (so called "All Risk" in American) coverage.
7. **Documentary implications**
   a. Commercial Documents: The seller should provide a commercial invoice, a packing list, and any other commercial documents cited in the sales contract.
   b. Transport Documents: The seller must provide a freight-prepaid transport document to the agreed place if requested by the buyer.
   c. Insurance Document: The seller should provide proof of insurance permitting the buyer or others with insurable interest to claim directly on the insurer.
   d. Export Control Documentation: The seller is obligated to handle export clearance under this Incoterms® rule. Since the seller usually selects the freight forwarder, it is also obligated to handle export reporting under the Census Foreign Trade Regulations. Note: for U.S. exports of reportable items, the value for EEI filing shall be the value of the goods in US dollars at the port, airport or land border of export (or the cost if not sold). See 15CFR Part 30.6(a)(17). Estimates are permitted.
   e. Import Entry Documentation: This is a buyer obligation. However, A7 requires the seller to provide assistance at the buyer's request, risk and cost.
8. **Payment terms considerations**
   By definition, the seller must arrange and pay for carriage to the agreed place. This means the seller is in a position to require the forwarder and carrier to provide transport documentation to its specifications, and will have access to them for use in both for letters of credit and documentary collections. The fact that the seller is also arranging insurance should provide additional comfort.

STORY LINE

Otto and Andre
Otto is a young importer of widgets located in Baden Baden, Germany. Andre is Otto's French widget supplier, located in Strasbourg, France, quite near the German border. Andre has blanket inland marine coverage which automatically attaches to his shipments. The cost is already factored in his selling prices.

Otto and Glotz
Otto wishes to purchase from Glotz Industries, a Fort Wayne widget manufacturer. Both are literally starting from scratch. After Otto rejected Glotz's EXW proposal, Glotz requoted using FCA. Otto requested another quotation on a freight-paid basis for comparison, to which Glotz added All Risk (Institute Clauses A) plus war, strike, riot and civil commotion cargo insurance at an attractive premium. They also obtained an attractive airport-to-door freight quotation enabling them to include the cost of on-carriage to Otto's premises. See Proforma invoice CIP 1.

Gordie and Glotz
This parallels Otto and Andre above.

Riddle and Glotz
Riddle always gets lower freight costs, and never purchases on a freight-prepaid basis.

AMERICAN VIEWPOINT

The seller is now required to provide the best standard coverage, Institute Cargo Clauses A (LMA/IUA) or its equivalent. This is what we Americans mistakenly call "All Risks" (and really should call "Almost All Risks"). Whatever name you use, it should be enhanced by Strike, Riot and Civil Commotion coverage and War coverage. You may also want to consider having it written on a Warehouse to Warehouse basis, which is the insurance jargon equivalent for door-to-door.

International use

This Incoterms® rule tasks the seller with export clearance. For US exporters, this is consistent with the Foreign Trade Regulations. The seller, known as the United States Principal Party in Interest (USPPI), is required to file the EEI or appoint an agent to do so, usually a seller-appointed forwarder. As the USPPI is contracting for transportation, it will have the necessary transportation information to file.

Delivery at the first carrier can cause problems for inexperienced users when pre-carriage is contracted independently of main carriage. Here's an extreme example. A "mom & pop" truck line was transporting an expensive yacht to a seaport for shipment against a port-to-port contract of main carriage. The truck crashed on the Indiana Toll Road and never reached the port. Sadly, mom, pop, the truck and the yacht are no more. As the seller has already delivered, upon whom does the foreign buyer claim? One answer would be the seller for failing to contract for main carriage because the yacht never arrived at the main carrier's terminal. The better answer would be an insurance company, provided the coverage is adequate and correctly written.

Since both the carrier and presumably the forwarder are working for the seller, there should be no problem obtaining documents necessary to make payment terms work. However, don't be surprised to receive letters of credit calling for "on board freight prepaid ocean bills of lading," extending the beneficiary's risk through vessel loading and resulting in a CIF-like situation. Many banks simply will not accept a "received for shipment" document, regardless of the fact that this agrees with the seller's CIP Incoterms® obligation. Others confuse the "on board-ness" with consignment instructions. It is perfectly possible to have a negotiable received for shipment marine transportation document. Fortunately, as the seller is contracting for main carriage, it is not terribly unreasonable that it be responsible for the carrier's loading obligations.

Another seller advantage is that each shipment made under C-Group Incoterms® rules is counted to its credit in negotiating shippers' agreements. Since the seller is the party contracting for transportation with the carrier, it is the shipper. Service providers respect VOLUME above all. Shippers that control many shipments have, do, and always will pay lower freight costs and get better service than less frequent shippers.

Experienced U.S. importers may prefer to buy on an F-Group term unless their suppliers offer exceptionally attractive freight costs. If this is the case, consider holding the seller responsible for the carrier it chooses by requesting DPU or DAP rather than C-Group rules. These rules also take the "first carrier" situation off the table. In any case, insist on proof of what the freight costs are (such as a rated transport document) to avoid paying import duty on inbound freight costs.

Depending on the stature of the buyer's insurance company and the currency of the contract, CIP buyers may want to consider obtaining contingency insurance. This is coverage issued by one insurer against the possibility of default by another.

Domestic use

Except for buyers attempting to achieve large shipper status, CIP presents no problem for purely domestic transactions.

CIP may present a minor issue for domestic use, as most coverage for domestic shipments is written under what is called inland marine coverage. Unlike marine cargo insurance used for international shipments, inland marine is normally written to automatically cover all domestic shipments over an agreed period for a fixed premium. The policy holder normally claims in case of damage or loss. However, the CIP Incoterms® rule specifies that the buyer or other parties with insurable interest must be able to claim directly from the insurer. This can usually be addressed by a seller commitment to file any necessary claims in the buyer's behalf.

PROFORMA INVOICE

EXPORTER Glotz Industries Inc 1492 Columbus Boulevard Fort Wayne, Indiana 12345-6789 USA	**PROFORMA INVOICE #** CIP 1	**PROFORMA INVOICE DATE** October 20, 2020
	PROFORMA VALIDITY DATE November 20, 2020	**EST'D SHIPMENT DATE** November 11, 2020
SOLD TO Widgets by Otto III Dean Haberkampstrasse Baden Baden GERMANY	**TERMS OF PAYMENT** Net 30 days	
	SHIPMENT/DELIVERY TERMS CIP Dean Haberkampstrasse, Baden Baden, Germany, Incoterms 2020	
SHIP TO Same as SOLD TO	**TITLE** Ownership transfers when payment is received by seller	

QUANTITY	UNITS	DESCRIPTION OF MERCHANDISE	UNIT PRICE	TOTAL
20	Each	Blue widgets	100.00	2000.00

LAW & DISPUTE RESOLUTION: The U.N. Convention on Contracts for the International Sale of Goods (1980) shall apply to this offer and any resulting contract. Any disputes will be resolved by binding arbitration services of the International Chamber of Commerce.

MERCHANDISE TOTAL	**US$** 2000.00
Export Packing	123.00
Pre carriage	138.00
Main carriage and On carriage	630.00
Insurance (All Risk, War, SRCC)	24.41
Forwarding	100.00
GRAND TOTAL CIP Baden Baden	**US$** 3015.41

CHAPTER 18 - COST AND FREIGHT

Abbreviation: CFR
Transport mode: vessel only
Contract type: shipment
Place: at the agreed port on the buyer's side

Cost and Freight (CFR) is a venerable shipment-delivery rule. Its correct use should be generally limited to non-containerized waterborne shipments where the seller contracts for main carriage and handles vessel loading.

Sellers deliver when the goods are on board the seller-appointed vessel. As "on board" is not defined, the parties should agree on exactly what this entails, particularly for charter movements. Tasks such as stowing and trimming are not specified

The seller's option of "procuring goods so delivered" is also mentioned in A2 to facilitate the use of this rule in commodity trade, where goods are commonly sold while in transit (so called "string sales"). This may be better understood as "providing goods so delivered."

CFR reflects the way most waterborne cargo was handled prior to containerization. Ports were little more than collections of piers to which outbound cargo was delivered for vessel loading. Nowadays, most modern ports are very secure areas. Outbound containerized cargo is normally handed over at facilities located some distance from the piers where the ships are actually loaded. Still, there are instances where CFR is appropriate:

- with vessel chartering, where the seller handles vessel loading and main carriage, as is common in commodity trades or with break-bulk shipments of project cargo,
- when the goods are sold after they have been loaded,
- with containers at small or less developed ports.

Despite the fact that its correct use is limited, it is unlikely that the CFR Incoterms®[49] rule will be deleted for many years to come. There are simply too many legacy issues.

The CFR rule is used for shipment contracts as the seller delivers when the goods are loaded on the vessel for shipment within the agreed time frame. This seems counterintuitive at first, as the place accompanying the rule is a port on the buyer's side of main carriage to which the seller contracts for main carriage. However, it is at vessel loading that the seller's risk ends, not where the goods finally arrive.

The CFR rule does not address vessel unloading. Sellers should carefully contract for transportation to match the agreed point at the agreed place, since buyers are not required to reimburse them for any additional costs beyond that point. Since there is no consistency as to how and to whom carriers charge unloading and terminal handling costs at destination ports, the parties should address this in their sales contract and sellers should contract for transportation accordingly.

The seller must notify the buyer that the goods have been loaded so that the buyer can make arrangements to collect them on arrival.

International shipments are accommodated since sellers are responsible for export clearance. This is consistent with "standard transactions" under Census' Foreign Trade Regulations.

[49] Incoterms® is a trademark of the International Chamber of Commerce, registered in several countries.

Since the seller is contracting for carriage, it usually also appoints the forwarder for international transactions. This enables the seller to provide instructions to these parties without the risk of their following any conflicting instructions from the buyer.

BUYER-SELLER RESPONSIBILITIES

The following is a short list of responsibilities.

1. **Goods and Payment**
   The seller must contract for transportation for shipment within the agreed time frame. The buyer must pay the seller.
   Since the seller is arranging transport, it should be aware of what packaging is needed.
2. **Loading and unloading**
   The seller is responsible for loading the goods onto the vessel.
3. **Pre-carriage and main carriage**
   Pre-carriage and contracting for and paying for main carriage are seller responsibilities under this rule.
4. **Export clearance**
   This is a seller responsibility under this rule.
5. **Other hoops and hurdles**
   The seller is responsible for compliance with any transport security regulations through delivery. The parties must work together on cargo security information. Since security regulations change often and vary from country to country and from one transport mode to another, Incoterms® rules are limited to making the parties aware that they must be addressed. This is covered in A4-B4 and A7-B7.
6. **Insurance**
   Neither party is required to insure. However, common sense dictates otherwise, and insurance should be addressed outside of the rule. Sellers are at risk until the goods are placed on board the vessel (check with your insurers about FAS/FOB coverage). Buyers are at risk thereafter.
7. **Documentary implications**
   a. Commercial Documents: The seller should provide a commercial invoice, a packing list, and any other commercial documents cited in the sales contract.
   b. Transport Documents: The seller should provide evidence that the contract goods were loaded on the vessel. This should usually be an "on board freight prepaid" marine transport document.
   c. Export Control Documentation: The seller is obligated to handle export clearance. Since the seller usually selects the forwarder, it is also obligated to handle export reporting under the Census Foreign Trade Regulations. Note: for U.S. exports of reportable items, the value for EEI filing shall be the value of the goods in US dollars at the port, airport or land border of export (or the cost if not sold). See 15CFR Part 30.6(a)(17). Estimates are permitted.
   d. Import Entry Documentation: This is a buyer obligation. However, A7 requires the seller to provide assistance at the buyer's request, risk and cost.
8. **Payment terms considerations**
   By definition, the seller must arrange for loading the goods onto the vessel. The only appropriate document would be one indicating that the goods are "on board." Since the seller is contracting for transportation, it would be freight prepaid. This document could easily be used to trigger a letter of credit. If issued in negotiable form (consigned to "order") it can also be used for documentary collections.

STORY LINE

None of the "usual suspects" would dream of using the CFR Incoterms® rule in day-to-day business. However, Glotz had some very large surplus equipment that was in good condition. It couldn't achieve the production economies needed for North America, but could be perfectly useful in a smaller market with lower labor costs. A Vietnamese manufacturer heard about it through a Japanese machinery broker and determined that it would suit his fledging operation. Glotz's forwarder found a U.S. company that regularly chartered shipments to Vietnam, usually with available excess capacity. Glotz obtained a low freight cost and quoted CFR Vung Tao Port, Vietnam and the buyer accepted.

Glotz subchartered space on a Vietnam bound vessel. Payment was by means of a confirmed irrevocable letter of credit requiring presentation of a clean on board freight prepaid bill of lading. Since payment was covered by an irrevocable confirmed letter of credit, Glotz was not concerned about providing insurance beyond vessel loading, and buried the modest cost of FAS/FOB coverge in the price of the machinery.[50] See Proforma CFR 1

Now aware of Glotz's activities through the above transaction, the machinery broker offered a late model good condition widget folding machine which was also too large for a container. The price was right and the Japanese seller offered a very low freight cost. Glotz ordered it on CFR Cleveland Port and irrevocable letter of credit terms, preferring to obtain insurance coverage here from a U.S. company. See Proforma CFR 2 (The fact that Glotz bought Institute clauses A plus war and strike coverage is irrelevant to this example.)

AMERICAN VIEWPOINT

Quite a bit of cargo moves by chartered vessel in terms of tonnage. Bulk commodities are usually transported this way (although container imbalances have made U.S. produce exporters aware of the benefits of containers). Huge pieces of project cargo too large for containers are shipped this way. These shipments require detailed planning and execution by all parties. CFR works particularly well for products typically loaded by sellers from pierside facilities, such as liquids from tank farms, grain from elevators, etc. Savvy American buyers usually prefer to insure here as U.S. insurers have a good record of honoring claims and pay them here in dollars.

International use

This Incoterms® rule tasks the seller with export clearance. For US exporters, this is consistent with the Foreign Trade Regulations. The seller, known as the United States Principal Party in Interest (USPPI), is required to file the EEI or appoint an agent to do so, usually a seller-appointed forwarder. As the USPPI is contracting for transportation, it will have the necessary transportation information to file.

Banks are quite attached to "on board ocean bills of lading." This is consistent with normal CFR documentation.

For chartering, the fact that the seller selects the main carrier may not be so important for purely volume considerations. Charter shipments are often negotiated individually, largely depending on vessel availability for the desired ports and times. However, for non-charter movements VOLUME is king, and sellers seeking large shipper status are helped by shipments on C-Group rules.

Experienced U.S. importers may prefer to buy on an F-Group rule unless their suppliers offer exceptionally attractive freight costs. If this is the case, consider holding the seller responsible for the performance of the carrier it chooses by requesting DAT or DAP rather than C-Group rules. In any case, insist on proof of what

---

[50] However, Glotz ignored the admittedly remote possibility of a general average situation.

the freight costs are such as a rated transport document to avoid paying import duty on inbound freight costs.

Domestic use

Used correctly the CFR Incoterms® 2020 rule presents no problem for purely domestic transactions. Barge movements come to mind, and there is growing interest in "short-sea" shipments from one U.S. port to another.

PROFORMA INVOICE

EXPORTER Glotz Industries Inc 1492 Columbus Boulevard Fort Wayne, Indiana 12345-6789 USA	**PROFORMA INVOICE #** CFR 1 **PROFORMA INVOICE DATE** December 7, 2020 **PROFORMA VALIDITY DATE** December 31, 2020 **EST'D SHIPMENT DATE** December 22, 2020
SOLD TO Vietnam Widgets Ltd. 4 Nixon Way Ho Chi Minh City VIETNAM	**TERMS OF PAYMENT** Irrevocable, confirmed letter of credit, payable at sight **SHIPMENT/DELIVERY TERMS** CFR Vung Tao Port, Vietnam, Incoterms 2020
SHIP TO Vung Tao Port, VIETNAM	**TITLE** Ownership transfers when payment is received by seller

QUANTITY	UNITS	DESCRIPTION OF MERCHANDISE	UNIT PRICE	TOTAL
1	Each	Used, complete widget manufacturing machine serial # 718-56, tested and operating at seller's premises before disassembly and shipment	973,500.00	973,500.00

LAW & DISPUTE RESOLUTION: The U.N. Convention on Contracts for the International Sale of Goods (1980) shall apply to this offer and any resulting contract. Any disputes will be resolved by binding arbitration services of the International Chamber of Commerce.	**MERCHANDISE TOTAL** Export Packing Pre carriage to port Terminal handling Heavy lift & loading Forwarding Main carriage	**US$** 973500.00 7230.00 3192.00 625.00 6709.00 100.00 85500.00
	GRAND TOTAL CFR Vung Tao Port	**US$** 1,076,856.00

PROFORMA INVOICE

EXPORTER Nihon Machinery Brokerage 777 Suzuki Avenue Tokyo, 729 Japan	**PROFORMA INVOICE #** CFR 2
	PROFORMA INVOICE DATE January 17, 2020
	PROFORMA VALIDITY DATE February 28, 2020
	EST'D SHIPMENT DATE April 1, 2020
SOLD TO Glotz Industries, Inc. 1492 Columbus Boulevard Fort Wayne, IN 12345-6789	**TERMS OF PAYMENT** Irrevocable letter of credit, payable at sight
	SHIPMENT/DELIVERY TERMS CFR Cleveland Port, Incoterms 2020
SHIP TO Cuyahoga Terminal Wharf Cleveland Port USA	**TITLE** Ownership transfers when payment is received by seller

QUANTITY	**UNITS**	**DESCRIPTION OF MERCHANDISE**	**UNIT PRICE**	**TOTAL**
1	Each	Used, complete widget folding machine serial # 703, tested and operating at seller's premises before disassembly and shipment	128,000.00	128,000.00

LAW & DISPUTE RESOLUTION: The U.N. Convention on Contracts for the International Sale of Goods (1980) shall apply to this offer and any resulting contract. Any disputes will be resolved by binding arbitration services of the International Chamber of Commerce.

MERCHANDISE TOTAL	US$128,000.00
Export Packing	900.00
Pre carriage to port	2,100.00
Terminal handling	700.00
Heavy lift & loading	3,000.00
Forwarding	100.00
Main carriage	43,000.00
GRAND TOTAL CFR Cleveland Port	**US$** 177,800.00

CHAPTER 19 - COST INSURANCE AND FREIGHT

Abbreviation: CIF
Transport mode: vessel only
Contract type: shipment
Place: at the agreed port on the buyer's side

Cost Insurance and Freight (CIF) is a venerable shipment-delivery rule. Its correct use should be generally limited to non-containerized waterborne shipments where the seller contracts for main carriage and handles vessel loading.

Sellers deliver when the goods are on board the seller-appointed vessel. As "on board" is not defined in detail, the parties should agree on exactly what this entails, especially for charter movements. Tasks such as stowing and trimming are not specified.

The seller's option "of procuring goods so delivered" is also mentioned in A2 to facilitate the use of this rule in commodity trade, where goods are commonly sold while in transit (so called "string sales"). This may be better understood as "providing goods so delivered"

CIF reflects the way most waterborne cargo was handled prior to containerization. Ports were little more than collections of piers to which outbound cargo was delivered for vessel loading. Nowadays, most modern ports are very secure areas. Outbound containerized cargo is normally handed over some distance from the ships. Still, there are instances where CIF is appropriate:

- with vessel chartering, where the seller handles vessel loading and main carriage, as is common in commodity trades or with break-bulk shipments of project cargo,
- when the goods are sold after they have been loaded,
- with containers at small or less developed ports.

Despite the fact that its correct use is limited, it is unlikely that the CIF Incoterms®[51] rule will be deleted for many years to come. There are simply too many legacy issues.

The CIF rule is used for shipment contracts as the seller delivers when the goods are loaded on the vessel for shipment within the agreed time frame. This seems counterintuitive at first, as the place accompanying the rule is a port on the buyer's side of main carriage to which the seller contracts for main carriage. However, it is at vessel loading that the seller's risk ends, not where the goods finally arrive.

The CIF rule does not address vessel unloading. Sellers should carefully contract for transportation to match the agreed point at the agreed place, since buyers are not required to reimburse them for any additional costs beyond that point. Since there is no consistency as to how and to whom carriers charge unloading and terminal handling costs at destination ports, the parties should address this in their sales contract and sellers should contract for transportation accordingly.

The seller must notify the buyer that the goods have been loaded so that the buyer can make arrangements to collect them on arrival.

International shipments are accommodated since sellers are responsible for export clearance. This is consistent with "standard transactions" under Census' Foreign Trade Regulations.

---

[51] Incoterms® is a trademark of the International Chamber of Commerce, registered in several countries.

Since the seller is contracting for carriage, it usually also appoints the forwarder for international transactions. This enables the seller to provide instructions to these parties without the risk of their following any conflicting instructions from the buyer.

The CIF rule stipulates that the seller must provide insurance, but limits this obligation to minimum cover unless the parties agree otherwise. Minimum cover is what we Americans call Free of Particular Average (FPA) and most others call Institute Cargo Clauses C. Either way, this coverage is extremely limited, and the parties should consider providing for additional risks for most shipments.

BUYER-SELLER RESPONSIBILITIES

The following is a short list of responsibilities.

1. **Goods and Payment**
   The seller must contract for transportation for shipment within the agreed time frame. The buyer must pay the seller.
   Since the seller is arranging transport, it should be aware of what packaging is needed.
2. **Loading and unloading**
   The seller is responsible for loading the goods onto the vessel.
3. **Pre-carriage and main carriage**
   Pre-carriage and contracting for and paying for main carriage are seller responsibilities under this rule.
4. **Export clearance**
   This is a seller responsibility under this rule.
5. **Other hoops and hurdles**
   The seller is responsible for compliance with any transport security regulations through delivery. The parties must work together on cargo security information. Since security regulations change often and vary from country to country and from one transport mode to another, Incoterms® rules are limited to making the parties aware that they must be addressed. This is covered in A4-B4 and A7-B7.
6. **Insurance**
   The seller is required to provide at least minimum cover insurance (FPA American or Institute Cargo Clauses C). Additional coverage should be considered.
7. **Documentary implications**
   a. Commercial Documents: The seller should provide a commercial invoice, a packing list, and any other commercial documents cited in the sales contract.
   b. Transport Documents: The seller should provide evidence that the contract goods were loaded on the vessel. This should usually be an "on board freight prepaid" marine transport document.
   c. Insurance Document: The seller should provide proof of insurance permitting the buyer or others with insurable interest to claim directly on the insurer.
   d. Export Control Documentation: The seller is obligated to handle export clearance. Since the seller usually selects the forwarder, it is also obligated to handle reporting under the Census Foreign Trade Regulations. Note: for U.S. exports of reportable items, the value for EEI filing shall be the value of the goods in US dollars at the port, airport or land border of export (or the cost if not sold). See 15CFR Part 30.6(a)(17). Estimates are permitted.
   e. Import Entry Documentation: This is a buyer obligation. However, A7 requires the seller to provide assistance at the buyer's request, risk and cost.
8. **Payment terms considerations**
   By definition, the seller must arrange for loading the goods onto the vessel. The only appropriate document would be one indicating that the goods are "on board." Since the seller is contracting for transportation, it would be freight prepaid. This document could easily be used to trigger a letter of

credit. If issued in negotiable form (consigned to "order") it can also be used for documentary collections.

STORY LINE

None of the "usual suspects" would dream of using the CIF Incoterms® rule in day-to-day business. However, Glotz had some very large surplus equipment that was in good condition. It couldn't achieve the production economies needed for North America, but could be perfectly useful in a smaller market with lower labor costs. A Vietnamese manufacturer heard about it through a machinery broker and determined that it would suit his fledging operation.

As mentioned in the previous chapter, Glotz subchartered space on a Vietnam bound vessel. Payment was by means of a confirmed irrevocable letter of credit requiring presentation of a clean on board freight prepaid bill of lading. Glotz then realized that it was at risk for the general average peril, so it and the buyer agreed to change the sales contract from CFR to CIF. The letter of credit was increased by the insurance cost and amended to also require an insurance certificate covering Free of Particular Average (Institute Clauses C). See Proforma CIF 1. Since payment was covered by an irrevocable confirmed letter of credit, Glotz was not concerned about additional perils.

However, the buyer subsequently realized that it was at risk for the condition of the goods after vessel loading with only limited insurance coverage. The parties agreed to another letter of credit increase and the insurance document description was changed to All Risk (Institute Clauses A) plus war, strike, riot and civil commotion. See proforma CIF 2.

AMERICAN VIEWPOINT

Quite a bit of cargo moves by chartered vessel in terms of tonnage. Bulk commodities are usually transported this way (although container imbalances have made U.S. produce exporters aware of the benefits of containers). Huge pieces of project cargo too large for containers are shipped this way. These shipments require detailed planning and execution by all parties. CIF works particularly well for products typically loaded by sellers from pierside facilities, such as liquids from tank farms, grain from elevators, etc.

The default position for insurance under the CIF rule is Institute Clauses C, roughly equivalent to what Americans call "free of particular average." This coverage is very limited. As insurance is relatively inexpensive, sellers and buyers not infrequently agree to broader coverage.

International use

This Incoterms® rule tasks the seller with export clearance. For US exporters, this is consistent with the Foreign Trade Regulations. The seller, known as the United States Principal Party in Interest (USPPI), is required to file the EEI or appoint an agent to do so, usually a seller-appointed forwarder. As the USPPI is contracting for transportation, it will have the necessary transportation information to file.

Banks are quite attached to "on board ocean bills of lading." This is consistent with normal CIF transport documentation.

For chartering, the fact that the seller selects the main carrier may not be so important for purely volume considerations. Charter shipments are often negotiated individually, largely depending on vessel availability for the desired ports and times. However, for non-charter movements VOLUME is king, and sellers seeking large shipper status are helped by shipments on C-Group rules.

Experienced U.S. importers may prefer to buy on an F-Group rule unless their suppliers offer exceptionally attractive freight costs. If this is the case, consider holding the seller responsible for the performance of the carrier it chooses by requesting DPU or DAP rather than C-Group rules. In any case, insist on proof of what the freight costs are such as a rated transport document to avoid paying import duty on inbound freight costs.

Domestic use

Used correctly the CIF Incoterms® 2010 rule presents no serious problem for purely domestic transactions. Barge movements come to mind, and there is growing interest in "short-sea" shipments from one U.S. port to another.

PROFORMA INVOICE

EXPORTER Glotz Industries Inc 1492 Columbus Boulevard Fort Wayne, Indiana 12345-6789 USA	**PROFORMA INVOICE #** CIF 1	**PROFORMA INVOICE DATE** December 14, 2020
	PROFORMA VALIDITY DATE December 31, 2020	**EST'D SHIPMENT DATE** December 22, 2020
SOLD TO Vietnam Widgets Ltd. 4 Nixon Way Ho Chi Minh City VIETNAM	**TERMS OF PAYMENT** Irrevocable, confirmed letter of credit, payable at sight	
	SHIPMENT/DELIVERY TERMS CIF Vung Tao Port, Vietnam, Incoterms 2020	
SHIP TO Vung Tao Port, VIETNAM	**TITLE** Ownership transfers when payment is received by seller	

QUANTITY	UNITS	DESCRIPTION OF MERCHANDISE	UNIT PRICE	TOTAL
1	Each	Used, complete widget manufacturing machine serial # 718-56, tested and operating at seller's premises before disassembly and shipment	973,500.00	973,500.00

LAW & DISPUTE RESOLUTION: The U.N. Convention on Contracts for the International Sale of Goods (1980) shall apply to this offer and any resulting contract. Any disputes will be resolved by binding arbitration services of the International Chamber of Commerce.

MERCHANDISE TOTAL	**US$** 973500.00
Export Packing	7230.00
Pre carriage to port	3192.00
Terminal handling load port	625.00
Heavy lift & loading	6709.00
Forwarding	100.00
Main carriage	85500.00
Insurance (Free of Particular Average)	761.31
GRAND TOTAL	**US$**
CIF Vung Tao Port	1,077,617.31

PROFORMA INVOICE

EXPORTER Glotz Industries Inc 1492 Columbus Boulevard Fort Wayne, Indiana 12345-6789 USA	**PROFORMA INVOICE #** CIF 2 **PROFORMA INVOICE DATE** December 17, 2020 **PROFORMA VALIDITY DATE** December 31, 2020 **EST'D SHIPMENT DATE** December 22, 2020
SOLD TO Vietnam Widgets Ltd. 4 Nixon Way Ho Chi Minh City VIETNAM	**TERMS OF PAYMENT** Irrevocable, confirmed letter of credit, payable at sight **SHIPMENT/DELIVERY TERMS** CIF Vung Tao Port, Vietnam, Incoterms 2020
SHIP TO Vung Tao Port, VIETNAM	**TITLE** Ownership transfers when payment is received by seller

QUANTITY	UNITS	DESCRIPTION OF MERCHANDISE	UNIT PRICE	TOTAL
1	Each	Used, complete widget manufacturing machine serial # 718-56, tested and operating at seller's premises before disassembly and shipment	973,500.00	973,500.00

LAW & DISPUTE RESOLUTION: The U.N. Convention on Contracts for the International Sale of Goods (1980) shall apply to this offer and any resulting contract. Any disputes will be resolved by binding arbitration services of the International Chamber of Commerce.

MERCHANDISE TOTAL	**US$** 973500.00
Export Packing	7230.00
Pre carriage to port	3192.00
Terminal handling load port	625.00
Heavy lift & loading	6709.00
Forwarding	100.00
Main carriage	85500.00
Insurance (All Risk War & SRCC)	3661.31
GRAND TOTAL CIF Vung Tao Port	**US$** 1,080,517.31

CHAPTER 20 - D-GROUP RULES

There are three D-Group rules: DAP, DPU and DDP. All three may be used for all transport modes.

One of the two main characteristics that D-Group rules have in common is that the seller is responsible for main carriage. This means the seller selects and contracts with the main carrier. It usually means that the seller also selects the freight forwarder as the roles of carrier and forwarder have blended to the point where they are almost indistinguishable.

The second characteristic is that all D-Group rules are used in arrival contracts. Sellers deliver when the contract goods arrive at the agreed place on the buyer's side. For this reason, sellers usually commit to arrival times rather than shipment times.

SELLERS

D-Group rules allow sellers to contract for main carriage transportation in return for being responsible for the performance of the forwarders and carriers they select. This seems fair. D-Group rules provide a comfort level with items subject to specific export control or commercial diversion. Document-driven payment terms could be difficult as delivery happens on arrival but shipping documents indicate merely that the contract goods have been shipped. Sellers that frequently select carriers are in a position to negotiate favorable freight rates, thereby reducing the total cost to their customers or even creating freight-cost profit centers. Export reporting is a seller obligation, consistent with both "standard transactions" under the Foreign Trade Regulations and with the Incoterms® rule.

With D-Group rules there is more work than with F-Group rules and more risk than with C-Group rules. Although insurance is not a requirement under the D-Group rules, sellers should consider obtaining adequate coverage as they remain at risk for the condition of the goods through arrival. Unlike coverage for the CIP and CIF rules, insurance should be made payable to the seller rather than to the buyer. As insurance claiming often require a level of buyer cooperation, savvy sellers make this a requirement in their sales contracts.

BUYERS

For experienced buyers, D-Group rules are the next best choice to F-Group rules provided that the sellers provide attractively low freight costs. Buyer risk is far lower than with C-Group rules. (As sellers are required to cover any pre-arrival loss or damage, the risk becomes whether they are able to do so.) U.S. importers must rely heavily on their suppliers for information on shipments subject to Importer Security Filing (ISF) pre-shipment reporting requirements.

HINT

DAP + unloading = DPU, DAP + import clearance = DDP

CHAPTER 21 - DELIVERED AT PLACE

Abbreviation: DAP
Transport mode: all
Contract type: arrival
Place: an agreed place on the buyer's side of transportation, not unloaded

Delivered At Place can be used with any mode of transportation and either single carrier or multimodal. The place must be on the buyer's side of the transportation for which the seller contracts. Possibilities include an arrival point such as a port or airport, the buyer's premises, or anywhere else the parties agree as long as it is on the buyer's side. Since this is where the seller's risk and cost end, it should be spelled out in as much detail as possible.

Sellers should carefully contract for transportation to match the agreed point at the agreed place, since buyers are not required to reimburse them for any additional costs beyond that point. This omnimodal rule is so versatile that no destination place can be set as a default. The parties should address this in their sales contract and sellers should contract for transportation accordingly.

This term is used in arrival contracts, where the parties agree that the seller delivers when the contract goods arrive at the agreed place.

Since the seller is contracting for carriage, it usually also appoints the forwarder for international transactions. This enables the seller to provide instructions to these parties without the risk of their following any conflicting instructions from the buyer.

BUYER-SELLER RESPONSIBILITIES

The following is a short list of responsibilities.

1. **Goods and Payment**
   The seller must ship the goods so as to arrive when promised, and must promptly notify the buyer that they have done so. The buyer must pay the seller.
   Since the seller is arranging transport, and is responsible for the condition of the goods up to the agreed destination, it should be aware of what packaging is needed.
2. **Loading and unloading**
   The seller is responsible for loading the collecting conveyance, and the buyer is responsible for unloading the delivering conveyance.
3. **Pre-carriage and main carriage (and on-carriage?)**
   The seller is responsible for payment of carriage to the agreed place on the buyer's side.
4. **Export clearance**
   This is a seller responsibility under this rule.
5. **Other hoops and hurdles**
   The parties must work together on cargo security information. This usually means one party telling the other what is required and the other party providing it. Since security regulations change often and vary from country to country and from one transport mode to another, Incoterms®[52] rules are

[52] Incoterms® is a trademark of the International Chamber of Commerce, registered in several countries.

limited to making the parties aware that they must be addressed. This is covered in A4-B4 and A7-B7.

6. **Insurance**
   Neither party is required to insure under DAP. However, common sense dictates otherwise, and sellers should consider insurance outside of the rule.
7. **Documentary implications**
   a. Commercial Documents: The seller should provide a commercial invoice, a packing list, and any other commercial documents cited in the sales contract.
   b. Transport Documents: The seller must provide a document enabling the buyer to receive the goods. While this could be a freight-prepaid transport document, this is strictly speaking insufficient to prove delivery as it indicates only that shipment has been made, not that it has successfully arrived.
   c. Export Control Documentation: The seller is obligated to handle export clearance under both DAP and the Census Foreign Trade Regulations. Note: for U.S. exports of reportable items, the value for EEI filing shall be the value of the goods in US dollars at the port, airport or land border of export (or the cost if not sold). See 15CFR Part 30.6(a)(17). Estimates are permitted.
   d. Import Entry Documentation: This is a buyer obligation. However, A7 requires the seller to provide assistance at the buyer's request, risk and cost.
8. **Payment terms considerations**
   By definition, the seller must arrange and pay for carriage to the agreed place. It is in a position to require the forwarder and carrier to provide transport documentation to its specifications. While the parties could theoretically agree to a freight-paid transport document for documentary collections and letters of credit, this does not conclusively prove that the goods have arrived. On the other hand, a document issued on arrival would often be too late for use with letters of credit. Documentary collections would provide no protection to the seller as the buyer would have already received the goods.

STORY LINE

Otto and Andre
Otto is a young importer of widgets located in Baden Baden, Germany. Andre is Otto's French widget supplier, located in Strasbourg, France, quite near the German border. Although Otto has negotiated very good freight rates with a truck line serving Strassburg and Baden-Baden, Andre has an even better rate with a small package carrier which they use for very small shipments and next-day service and is willing to remain responsible for the condition of the goods until they arrive. See proforma DAP 1.

Otto and Glotz
Otto wishes to purchase from Glotz Industries, a Fort Wayne widget manufacturer. Both are literally starting from scratch. Glotz has already made price quotations on other Incoterms® rules without success. In an attempt to obtain at least a small first order and hopefully renew the old relationship, Glotz quoted DAP Otto's premises in Baden Baden . It is charging for insurance as shown as a separate line item. See proforma DAP 2.

Gordie and Glotz
Glotz has negotiated exceptionally low door-to-door freight costs with a carrier that provides service to Canada. Since there is no greater risk to the cargo in Canadian transit than here, and as shipments to Canada are automatically covered under their inland marine policy, Glotz is willing to remain responsible for the condition of the goods through delivery. Since Glotz is a privately held company, there is no investor pressure to recognize revenue at the earliest possible moment. See proforma DAP 3.

Jerry and Glotz
Glotz is not at all comfortable remaining responsible for the condition of the goods during transit within Mexico.

Riddle and Glotz
Riddle always gets lower freight costs, and never purchases on a freight-prepaid basis.

AMERICAN VIEWPOINT

International use
The DAP Incoterms® 2020 rule is used in arrival contracts where the seller delivers when the goods arrive at the agreed place on the buyer's side ready for unloading. The unloading logic is that the buyer is normally better positioned to unload than is the remote seller. Parties wishing the seller to be responsible for unloading should consider the new DPU rule.

This Incoterms® rule tasks the seller with export clearance. For US exporters, this is consistent with the Foreign Trade Regulations. The seller, known as the United States Principal Party in Interest (USPPI), is required to file the EEI or appoint an agent to do so, usually a seller-appointed forwarder. As the USPPI is contracting for transportation, it will have the necessary transportation information to file.

Another seller advantage is that each shipment made under D-Group Incoterms® rules is another that is counted to its credit in negotiating shippers' freight agreements. Since the seller is the party contracting for transportation with the carrier, it is the shipper. Service providers respect VOLUME above all. Shippers that control many shipments have, do, and always will pay lower freight costs and get better service than less frequent shippers.

Publicly traded corporations will find that the arrival nature of this rule can result in delayed revenue recognition.

Experienced U.S. importers may prefer to buy on an F-Group term unless their suppliers offer exceptionally attractive freight costs. In any case, insist on proof of what the freight costs are such as a rated transport document to avoid paying import duty on inbound freight costs.

Domestic use
This plays out the same as international use except for export clearance. It works well with the door-to-door ground transportation so prevalent here.

PROFORMA INVOICE

EXPORTER Les Widgets de France Rue John-Pierre Robin 12 Strasbourg FRANCE	**PROFORMA INVOICE #** DAP 1 **PROFORMA INVOICE DATE** November 8, 2020 **PROFORMA VALIDITY DATE** December 10, 2020 **EST'D SHIPMENT DATE** November 9, 2020
SOLD TO Widgets by Otto III Dean Haberkampstrasse Baden Baden GERMANY	**TERMS OF PAYMENT** Net 30 days **SHIPMENT/DELIVERY TERMS** DAP Dean Haberkampstrasse, Baden Baden, Germany, Incoterms 2020
SHIP TO Same as SOLD TO	**TITLE** Ownership transfers when payment is received by seller

QUANTITY	UNITS	DESCRIPTION OF MERCHANDISE	UNIT PRICE	TOTAL
2	Each	Bleu widgets	€ 100.00	200.00

LAW & DISPUTE RESOLUTION: The U.N. Convention on Contracts for the International Sale of Goods (1980) shall apply to this offer and any resulting contract. Any disputes will be resolved by binding arbitration services of the International Chamber of Commerce.	**MERCHANDISE TOTAL** Freight	€ 200.00 32.00
	GRAND TOTAL DAP Baden Baden	€ 232.00

PROFORMA INVOICE

EXPORTER Glotz Industries Inc 1492 Columbus Boulevard Fort Wayne, Indiana 12345-6789 USA	**PROFORMA INVOICE #** DAP 2	**PROFORMA INVOICE DATE** October 22, 2020
	PROFORMA VALIDITY DATE November 22, 2020	**EST'D SHIPMENT DATE** November 15, 2020
SOLD TO Widgets by Otto III Dean Haberkampstrasse Baden Baden GERMANY	**TERMS OF PAYMENT** Net 30 days	
	SHIPMENT/DELIVERY TERMS DAP Dean Haberkampstrasse, Baden Baden, Germany, Incoterms 2020	
SHIP TO Same as SOLD TO	**TITLE** Ownership transfers when payment is received by seller	

QUANTITY	UNITS	DESCRIPTION OF MERCHANDISE	UNIT PRICE	TOTAL
20	Each	Blue widgets	100.00	2000.00

LAW & DISPUTE RESOLUTION: The U.N. Convention on Contracts for the International Sale of Goods (1980) shall apply to this offer and any resulting contract. Any disputes will be resolved by binding arbitration services of the International Chamber of Commerce.

MERCHANDISE TOTAL	**US$** 2000.00
Export Packing	123.00
Pre carriage	138.00
Main carriage and On carriage	630.00
Insurance (A+ War & Strike)	24.41
Forwarding	100.00
GRAND TOTAL DAP Baden Baden	**US$** 3015.41

PROFORMA INVOICE

EXPORTER Glotz Industries Inc 1492 Columbus Boulevard Fort Wayne, Indiana 12345-6789 USA	**PROFORMA INVOICE #** DAP 3 **PROFORMA INVOICE DATE** October 19, 2020 **PROFORMA VALIDITY DATE** November 15, 2020 **EST'D SHIPMENT DATE** November 19, 2020
SOLD TO Gordie's Good Widgets 1 Carl Crewson Street North Bay, Ontario CANADA	**TERMS OF PAYMENT** Net 30 days **SHIPMENT/DELIVERY TERMS** DAP 1 Carl Crewson Street, North Bay, Ontario, Canada, Incoterms 2020
SHIP TO Same as SOLD TO	**TITLE** Ownership transfers when payment is received by seller

QUANTITY	UNITS	DESCRIPTION OF MERCHANDISE	UNIT PRICE	TOTAL
40	Each	Blue widgets	100.00	4000.00

LAW & DISPUTE RESOLUTION: The U.N. Convention on Contracts for the International Sale of Goods (1980) shall apply to this offer and any resulting contract. Any disputes will be resolved by binding arbitration services of the International Chamber of Commerce.	**MERCHANDISE TOTAL** Freight	**US$** 4000.00 392.00
	GRAND TOTAL DAP North Bay	**US$** 4,392.00

CHAPTER 22 - DELIVERED AT PLACE UNLOADED

Abbreviation: DPU
Transport mode: all
Contract type: arrival
Place: an agreed location on the buyer's side of transportation - unloaded

The Delivered at Place Unloaded rule is new for 2020. It replaced the former Delivered At Terminal (which itself replaced the former Delivered Ex Quay rule in 2010). DPU can be used with any mode of transportation and either single carrier or multimodal. The place must be on the buyer's side of the transportation for which the seller contracts. Possibilities include a quay next to an arriving vessel at an arrival port, an airport, a truck terminal, a container yard, a container de-consolidator, or another agreed location such as a jobsite. Since this is where the seller's risk and cost end, it should be spelled out in as much detail as possible.

The distinguishing characteristic of this rule is that alone among the 2020 rules it requires the seller to unload the contract goods. Sellers should carefully contract for transportation to match the agreed point at the agreed place, since buyers are not required to reimburse them for any additional costs beyond that point. This omnimodal rule is so versatile that no destination place can be set as a default. In some situations, the parties may agree to a location some distance from the arrival point on the buyer's side, and on-carriage providers may not typically provide unloading. Since there is no consistency as to how and to whom carriers levy these charges, the parties should carefully address this issue in their sales contract.

This term is used in arrival contracts, where the parties agree that the seller delivers when the contract goods are unloaded at the agreed place.

Since the seller is contracting for carriage, it usually also appoints the forwarder for international transactions. This enables the seller to provide instructions to these parties without the risk of their following any conflicting instructions from the buyer.

BUYER-SELLER RESPONSIBILITIES

The following is a short list of responsibilities.

1. **Goods and Payment**
   The seller must ship the goods so as to arrive when promised, and must promptly notify the buyer that they have done so. The buyer must pay the seller.
   Since the seller is arranging transport, and is responsible for the condition of the contract goods through unloading, it should be aware of what packaging is needed.
2. **Loading and unloading**
   The seller is responsible for both loading and unloading.
3. **Pre-carriage and main carriage (and on-carriage?)**
   The seller is responsible for payment of carriage to the agreed place on the buyer's side.
4. **Export clearance**
   This is a seller responsibility under this rule.
5. **Other hoops and hurdles**
   The seller is responsible for compliance with any transport security regulations through delivery. The parties must work together on cargo security information. Since security regulations change often and vary from country to country and from one transport mode to another, Incoterms® rules are limited to making the parties aware that they must be addressed. This is covered in A4-B4 and A7-B7.

6. **Insurance**
   Neither party is required to insure under DPU. However, common sense dictates otherwise, and sellers should consider insurance outside of the rule.
7. **Documentary implications**
   a. Commercial Documents: The seller should provide a commercial invoice, a packing list, and any other commercial documents cited in the sales contract.
   b. Transport Documents: The seller must provide a document enabling the buyer to receive the goods. While this could be a freight-prepaid transport document, this is strictly speaking insufficient as it indicates only that shipment has been made, not that it has successfully arrived.
   c. Export Control Documents: The seller is obligated to handle export clearance. Since the seller usually selects the freight forwarder, it is also obligated to handle export reporting under the Census Foreign Trade Regulations. Note: for U.S. exports of reportable items, the value for EEI filing shall be the value of the goods in US dollars at the port, airport or land border of export (or the cost if not sold). See 15CFR Part 30.6(a)(17). Estimates are permitted.
   d. Import Entry Documentation: This is a buyer obligation. However, A7 requires the seller to provide assistance at the buyer's request, risk and cost.
8. **Payment terms considerations**
   By definition, the seller must arrange and pay for carriage to the agreed place. It is in a position to require the forwarder and carrier to provide transport documentation to its specifications. While the parties could theoretically agree to a freight-paid transport document for documentary collections and letters of credit, this does not conclusively prove that the goods have arrived. On the other hand, a document issued on arrival would often be too late for use with letters of credit. Documentary collections would provide little protection to the seller, and then only if the goods were to be delivered to a terminal or a container de-consolidator. Obviously, there would be no protection at all if the buyer would have already received the goods.

STORY LINE

Otto and Andre
Otto is a young importer of widgets located in Baden Baden, Germany. Andre is Otto's French widget supplier, located in Strasbourg, France, quite near the German border. They never use this rule as Otto always has employees available to unload any incoming shipments that he doesn't pick up at Andre's premises.

Otto and Glotz
Otto is now purchasing from Glotz Industries, a Fort Wayne widget manufacturer. Both are literally starting from scratch. Occasionally, Otto orders for shipment by vessel in less than full container load quantities (LCL) using the DPU rule. When the container arrives, the carrier unloads and separates each consignee's goods for pick up. See proforma DPU 1. Since Glotz is a privately held company, there is no investor pressure to recognize revenue at the earliest possible moment.

Gordie and Glotz
Gordie either brings the widgets to his premises himself or always has personnel to unload incoming shipments.

Jerry and Glotz
These parties never use the DPU rule. They have been using FCA Laredo for years with no problems.

Riddle and Glotz
Riddle always gets lower freight costs, and never purchases on a freight-prepaid basis.

The Cutting Edge Manufacturing Company and Glotz
As the name implies Cutting Edge produces precision measuring equipment permitting high volume widget manufacturing. Its equipment must be carefully handled in transit, correctly installed and calibrated. For this reason, they ship in specially configured air freight containers which they insist be unloaded by their own personnel on site. The DPU rule addresses this unusual situation perfectly. See proforma DPU 2.

The Furna Hotel
The Furna Hotel and Resort is located on the island of Brava, Cape Verde Islands. This area has lately become a popular tourist haven. Its port is too shallow to accommodate most vessels, so shipments are handled by a barge traveling between the port and visiting geared[53] ships at anchor. The hotel's standby generator shorted out while under warranty, and the manufacturer sent a replacement. Proforma DPU 3 shows the necessary vessel unloading for lighterage.

AMERICAN VIEWPOINT

International use
This new Incoterms®[54] 2020 rule is used in arrival contracts where the seller delivers by unloading at an agreed destination and is the only rule that specifically tasks the seller with unloading.

It works well with carriage contracts that include unloading. However, the parties must take care that the buyer isn't also charged with associated costs which were already covered in the prepaid transportation contract provided by the seller. This requires constant attention as there is no consistency in the way such costs are charged.

DPU can work well with shipments by small package carriers whose drivers typically unload their own vehicles. Consolidated container loads where individual shipments are unloaded and placed at the disposal of their consignees by a de-consolidator is another obvious use. Another possibility is for breakbulk shipments on geared vessels to ports with limited facilities where the unloading is handled by the vessel itself. A fourth would be for vessel shipments to shallow ports where vessel unloading to a barge is required. DPU could also work for delivery at a jobsite where the parties want the seller to unload the delivering conveyance.

This Incoterms® rule tasks the seller with export clearance. For US exporters, this is consistent with the Foreign Trade Regulations. The seller, known as the United States Principal Party in Interest (USPPI), is required to file the EEI or appoint an agent to do so, usually a seller-appointed forwarder. As the USPPI is contracting for transportation, it will have the necessary transportation information to file.

Another seller advantage is that each shipment made under D-Group Incoterms® rules is another that is counted to its credit in negotiating shippers' freight agreements. Since the seller is the party contracting for transportation with the carrier, it is the shipper. Service providers respect VOLUME above all. Shippers that control many shipments have, do, and always will pay lower freight costs and get better service than less frequent shippers.

Publicly traded corporations will find that the arrival nature of this rule can result in delayed revenue recognition.

---

[53] A geared vessel is one with lifting capacity, i.e. a crane.

[54] Incoterms® is a trademark of the International Chamber of Commerce, registered in several countries.

Experienced U.S. importers may prefer to buy on an F-Group term unless their suppliers offer exceptionally attractive freight costs. In any case, insist on proof of what the freight costs are such as a rated transport document to avoid paying import duty on inbound freight costs.

Domestic use

This plays out the same as international use except for export clearance.

PROFORMA INVOICE

EXPORTER Glotz Industries Inc 1492 Columbus Boulevard Fort Wayne, Indiana 12345-6789 USA	**PROFORMA INVOICE #** DPU 1	**PROFORMA INVOICE DATE** October 20, 2020
	PROFORMA VALIDITY DATE November 20, 2020	**EST'D SHIPMENT DATE** November 11, 2020
SOLD TO Widgets by Otto III Dean Haberkampstrasse Baden Baden GERMANY	**TERMS OF PAYMENT** Net 30 days	
	SHIPMENT/DELIVERY TERMS DPU Consolidated Container Warehouse, Markus Duengerstrasse 11, Frankfurt, Germany, Incoterms 2020	
SHIP TO Same as SOLD TO	**TITLE** Ownership transfers when payment is received by seller	

QUANTITY	UNITS	DESCRIPTION OF MERCHANDISE	UNIT PRICE	TOTAL
20	Each	Blue widgets	100.00	2000.00

LAW & DISPUTE RESOLUTION: The U.N. Convention on Contracts for the International Sale of Goods (1980) shall apply to this offer and any resulting contract. Any disputes will be resolved by binding arbitration services of the International Chamber of Commerce.	**MERCHANDISE TOTAL** Export Packing Pre carriage Main carriage Insurance (A+ War & Strike) Forwarding	**US$** 2000.00 123.00 138.00 630.00 24.41 100.00
	GRAND TOTAL DPU Frankfurt	**US$** 3015.41

PROFORMA INVOICE

EXPORTER Cutting Edge Manufacturing Company 1066 Senlac Court Birmingham BR216GB United Kingdom	**PROFORMA INVOICE #** DPU 2 **PROFORMA INVOICE DATE** May 2, 2020 **PROFORMA VALIDITY DATE** June 3, 2020 **EST'D SHIPMENT DATE** August 15, 2020
SOLD TO Glotz Industries Inc 1492 Columbus Boulevard Fort Wayne, Indiana 12345-6789 USA	**TERMS OF PAYMENT** 70% with order, remainder net upon installation, US Dollars **SHIPMENT/DELIVERY TERMS** DPU 1492 Columbus Boulevard, Fort Wayne, Indiana USA, Incoterms 2020
SHIP TO Same as SOLD TO	**TITLE** Ownership transfers when full payment is received by seller

QUANTITY	UNITS	DESCRIPTION OF MERCHANDISE	UNIT PRICE	TOTAL
1	Each	Measure Master model 308 precision guide, squaring and leveling device In addition to this price, buyer will reimburse travel and subsistence cost for one technician for 3 working days. Carriage is closely controlled door-to-door. Technician will arrive at Fort Wayne one day before delivery to unload and install.	$ 81,000.00	$ 81,000.00

LAW & DISPUTE RESOLUTION: The U.N. Convention on Contracts for the International Sale of Goods (1980) shall apply to this offer and any resulting contract. Any disputes will be resolved by binding arbitration services of the International Chamber of Commerce.	**MERCHANDISE TOTAL** Export Packing Air freight door-door Main carriage and On carriage Insurance (A+ War & Strike) Unloading & Installation	US$ 81,000.00 3,123.00 2,725.00 630.00 175.41 6,100.00
	GRAND TOTAL DPU Fort Wayne, installed	**US$** 93,753.41

PROFORMA INVOICE

EXPORTER Zap Electrics Ltd. 7 Queen Victoria Parade Belfast NO72OK United Kingdom	**PROFORMA INVOICE #** DPU 3 **PROFORMA INVOICE DATE** September 20, 2020 **PROFORMA VALIDITY DATE** October 1, 2020 **EST'D SHIPMENT DATE** September 21, 2020
SOLD TO Furna Hotel & Resort Prominade Brava Capt Verde Islands	**TERMS OF PAYMENT** No Charge – Replacement of defective generator **SHIPMENT/DELIVERY TERMS** DPU barge alongside Vessel Hesperus, Incoterms 2020
SHIP TO Shipside, offshore at Port Brava entrance	**TITLE** Warranty return

QUANTITY	**UNITS**	**DESCRIPTION OF MERCHANDISE**	**UNIT PRICE**	**TOTAL**
1	Each	Standby generator replaced under warranty. Value for customs purposes original price of Lstg. 8,780.00	No charge	0.00

LAW & DISPUTE RESOLUTION: The U.N. Convention on Contracts for the International Sale of Goods (1980) shall apply to this offer and any resulting contract. Any disputes will be resolved by binding arbitration services of the International Chamber of Commerce.	**MERCHANDISE TOTAL**	0.00
	GRAND TOTAL DPU barge, Brava, Cape Verde Is.	0.00

CHAPTER 23 - DELIVERED DUTY PAID

Abbreviation: DDP
Transport mode: all
Contract type: arrival
Place: an agreed place on the buyer's side of transportation

Delivered Duty Paid can be used with any mode of transportation and either single carrier or multimodal. The place must be on the buyer's side of the transportation for which the seller contracts. Possibilities include an arrival point such as a port or airport, the buyer's premises, or anywhere else the parties agree as long as it is on the buyer's side. The time and place for customs clearance may also affect place selection. Since this is where the seller's risk and cost end, it should be spelled out in as much detail as possible.

Sellers should carefully contract for transportation to match the agreed point at the agreed place, since buyers are not required to reimburse them for any additional costs beyond that point. This omnimodal rule is so versatile that no destination place can be set as a default. The parties should address this in their sales contract and sellers should contract for transportation accordingly.

This term is used in arrival contracts, where the parties agree that the seller delivers when the contract goods arrive at the agreed place. Alone among the Incoterms®[55] 2020 rules, it requires the seller to handle and pay for import clearance, and as such represents the maximum seller obligation. Any applicable value added taxes are also for the seller's account unless the parties agree otherwise. This seems counterintuitive. VAT is sometimes refundable under certain circumstances, and buyers would more likely be aware of how this works in their own countries.

Since the seller is contracting for carriage, it usually also appoints the forwarder for international transactions. This enables the seller to provide instructions to these parties without the risk of their following any conflicting instructions from the buyer. As the seller is also responsible for import clearance, it also will normally engage a customs broker in the buyer's country.

BUYER-SELLER RESPONSIBILITIES

The following is a short list of responsibilities.

1. **Goods and Payment**
   The seller must ship the goods so as to arrive when promised, and must promptly notify the buyer that they have done so. The buyer must pay the seller.
   Since the seller is arranging transport, and is responsible for the condition of the goods up to the agreed destination, it should be aware of what packaging is needed.
2. **Loading and unloading**
   The seller is responsible for loading the collecting conveyance, and the buyer is responsible for unloading the delivering conveyance.
3. **Pre-carriage and main carriage (and on-carriage?)**
   The seller is responsible for payment of carriage to the agreed place on the buyer's side.

[55] Incoterms® is a trademark of the International Chamber of Commerce, registered in several countries.

4. **Export clearance and import clearance**
   Both are seller responsibilities under this rule.
5. **Other hoops and hurdles**
   The parties must work together on cargo security information. This usually means one party telling the other what is required and the other party providing it. Since security regulations change often and vary from country to country and from one transport mode to another, Incoterms® rules are limited to making the parties aware that they must be addressed. This is covered in A4-B4 and A7-B7.
6. **Insurance**
   Neither party is required to insure under DDP. However, common sense dictates otherwise, and the seller should consider insurance outside of the rule.
7. **Documentary implications**
   a. Commercial Documents: The seller should provide a commercial invoice, a packing list, and any other commercial documents cited in the sales contract.
   b. Transport Documents: The seller must provide a document enabling the buyer to receive the goods. While this could be a freight-prepaid transport document, this is strictly speaking insufficient as it indicates only that shipment has been made, not that it has successfully arrived.
   c. Export Control Documentation: The seller is obligated to handle export clearance under both DDP and the Foreign Trade Regulations. Note: for U.S. exports of reportable items, the value for EEI filing shall be the value of the goods in US dollars at the port, airport or land border of export (or the cost if not sold). See 15CFR Part 30.6(a)(17). Estimates are permitted.
   d. Import Entry Documentation: As this is a seller obligation, the seller should provide the buyer with evidence of import clearance and duty payment. However, B7 requires the buyer to provide assistance at the seller's request, risk and cost.
8. **Payment terms considerations**
   By definition, the seller must arrange and pay for carriage to the agreed place and handle import clearance. It is in a position to require the forwarder and carrier to provide transport documentation to its specifications. While the parties could theoretically agree to a freight-paid transport document for documentary collections and letters of credit, this does not conclusively prove that the goods have arrived or that they have been cleared for import. On the other hand, a document issued on arrival indicating import clearance would often be too late for use with letters of credit. Documentary collections would provide no protection to the seller as the buyer would have already received the goods. Further, as the goods would have already entered the commerce of the buyer's country, the seller's chances of reclaiming them are slim. For these reasons, DDP is best suited to payment with order, open account, or standby letter of credit terms.

STORY LINE

Otto and Andre

Otto is a young importer of widgets located in Baden Baden, Germany who purchases from Andre, a French manufacturer. As they are both in the European Union, DAP and DDP are about the same except for the VAT. As this is best handled by Otto, they do not use this rule.

Otto and Glotz

Glotz's third shipment was an unmitigated disaster. The widgets looked fine, but didn't work. This was discovered only after Otto's best customer began to use them in its manufacturing process. Result is that an entire production line is down and, German labor law being what it is, the workers continue receiving their full pay. Being a responsible supplier, Glotz is willing to move heaven and earth to make things as right as they can. They come close to doing exactly that by shipping replacements at no charge by air freight. Rather than further inconveniencing Otto, they used DDP and sent Otto the no charge invoice DDP 1.

Gordie and Glotz
Being of sound mind, the parties have agreed that just because it is possible to be a "non-resident-importer" is no reason that this should be done.

Jerry and Glotz
No way would Glotz become involved in Mexican import clearance, even if they could.

Thai Pride and U.S. retailers
Thai Pride is a small metals manufacturer located near Bangkok. They have found a use for small base metal scrap sections by stamping them into picture frames embossed with a picture of the King of Thailand and Thai flags aimed at the Thai community in major U.S. cities. They had been offering them through an importing distributor who resold to retailers. Because of the recently increased U.S. import de-minimis amount, they can now instead sell directly online to local retailers. They must be careful not to exceed the one shipment per customer per day rule and the maximum $800 merchandise value per shipment. This really isn't a problem as the retailer-customers seldom buy more than fifty frames at a time. See proforma DDP 2.

Riddle and Glotz
Not applicable as Glotz supplies only U.S. made widgets.

AMERICAN VIEWPOINT

International use
This Incoterms® 2020 rule is little changed from its 2010 predecessor, and continues to make as little sense for Americans. It is used in arrival contracts where the seller delivers when the goods arrive at the agreed place on the buyer's side, import cleared and ready for unloading. The unloading logic is the same as found in FCA + other location and DAP in that the buyer is normally better positioned to unload than is the remote seller.

This Incoterms® rule tasks the seller with export clearance. For US exporters, this is consistent with the Foreign Trade Regulations. The seller, known as the United States Principal Party in Interest (USPPI), is required to file the EEI or appoint an agent to do so, usually a seller-appointed forwarder. As the USPPI is contracting for transportation, it will have the necessary transportation information to file.

DDP also tasks the seller with import clearance. This writer remains unconvinced that the seller is ever better positioned to deal with the buyer's country than the buyer is. Readers who consider exporting under this term may want to answer the following questions:

1. Are you sure you know how import clearance is done in the buyer's country?
2. Are you sure you know the correct duty rate, and can it change?
3. Do you know how to select a customs broker in the buyer's country, and how much they charge?
4. Are you incurring contingent liability to a foreign government?
5. Could you be considered "doing business" in the destination country and become subject to local taxes beyond those applicable to the actual import?
6. Could you unwittingly run afoul of U.S. Foreign Corrupt Practices Act violations when your appointed foreign customs broker follows "normal" local practice vis-à-vis local government officials.
7. Does the buyer's government want to deal with you?
8. Will your transactions stand out and invite greater than normal scrutiny?
9. How would you arrange the return of unwanted or unpaid product that has already been import cleared?

Each shipment made under D-Group Incoterms® rules is another that is counted to its credit in negotiating shippers' agreements. Since the seller is the party contracting for transportation with the carrier, it is the shipper. Service providers respect VOLUME above all. Shippers that control many shipments have, do, and always will pay lower freight costs and get better service than less frequent shippers. However, this can be accomplished by more seller-friendly Incoterms® rules.

Publicly traded corporations will find that the arrival nature of this rule can result in delayed revenue recognition, and may prefer to use C-Group rules. Their accountants also will just love any contingent liability remaining until DDP shipments are finally liquidated in the buyers' countries.

Experienced U.S. importers may prefer to buy on an F-Group term unless their suppliers offer exceptionally attractive freight costs. Even then, they should opt for DAP rather than DDP. Reasons include:

1. Any sane overseas seller will be as concerned about U.S. import clearance as we would be about theirs. There will very likely be a premium buried in the price for potential risk.
2. Compliance will depend on the competence of a U.S. customs broker appointed by a foreign supplier. Some brokers are better than others!
3. Occasionally, Customs may have a routine question which the buyer could readily address if it were the importer of record. However, with DDP, the buyer is not a party to import clearance.
4. Any drawback claims would be needlessly complicated, and would require cooperation of the foreign seller.

A few possible reasons for sellers and buyers using DDP come to mind:

1. Replacement parts for warranty work.
2. Small low-value shipments below the de-minimis value of the importing country.
3. No-charge sample and literature.
4. Trade within a customs union.
5. Desperate sellers at buyer insistence when abnormally high import duty threatens. (Caution here!)
6. Support for service personnel operating far from population centers (such as oil exploration).

Domestic use

While DDP may lend itself to domestic sales of pre-imported, pre-cleared goods on which any applicable duty has already been paid and presumably included in the price of the goods themselves, DAP is a better choice. The possible misuse of DDP in international situations argues for keeping it away from domestic parties who are unfamiliar with the way Incoterms® rules work.

PROFORMA INVOICE

EXPORTER Glotz Industries Inc 1492 Columbus Boulevard Fort Wayne, Indiana 12345-6789 USA	**PROFORMA INVOICE #** DDP 1	**PROFORMA INVOICE DATE** October 22, 2020	
	PROFORMA VALIDITY DATE November 22, 2020	**EST'D SHIPMENT DATE** November 15, 2020	
SOLD TO Widgets by Otto III Dean Haberkampstrasse Baden Baden GERMANY	**TERMS OF PAYMENT** No Charge – Value for Customs purposes only		
	SHIPMENT/DELIVERY TERMS DDP Dean Haberkampstrasse, Baden Baden, Germany, Incoterms 2020		
SHIP TO Same as SOLD TO	**TITLE** Buyer to own these warranty replacement goods upon arrival.		

QUANTITY	UNITS	DESCRIPTION OF MERCHANDISE	UNIT PRICE	TOTAL
20	Each	Blue widgets WARRANTY REPLACEMENT OF DEFECTIVE GOODS	100.00	2000.00

LAW & DISPUTE RESOLUTION: The U.N. Convention on Contracts for the International Sale of Goods (1980) shall apply to this offer and any resulting contract. Any disputes will be resolved by binding arbitration services of the International Chamber of Commerce.	**MERCHANDISE TOTAL**	**US$** 2000.00
	Export Packing	123.00
	Pre carriage	138.00
	Main carriage and On carriage	630.00
	Insurance (A+ War & Strike)	24.41
	Forwarding	100.00
	Import Clearance	350.00
	GRAND TOTAL DDP Baden Baden	**US$** 3365.41

PROFORMA INVOICE

EXPORTER Thai Pride 200 Paiboon Bencharit Road Bangkok, Thailand	**PROFORMA INVOICE #** DDP 2 **PROFORMA INVOICE DATE** October 10, 2020 **PROFORMA VALIDITY DATE** November 10, 2020 **EST'D SHIPMENT DATE** November 1, 2020
SOLD TO Thai Things 31 Santa Ana Street Los Angeles, CA USA	**TERMS OF PAYMENT** Credit card **SHIPMENT/DELIVERY TERMS** DDP Thai Things, 31 Santa Ana St. Los Angeles, California, Incoterms 2020
SHIP TO Same as SOLD TO	**TITLE** Ownership transfers when goods are received by buyer.

QUANTITY	UNITS	DESCRIPTION OF MERCHANDISE	UNIT PRICE	TOTAL
50	Each	Picture frames with THAI flags	5.00	250.00

LAW & DISPUTE RESOLUTION: The U.N. Convention on Contracts for the International Sale of Goods (1980) shall apply to this offer and any resulting contract. Any disputes will be resolved by binding arbitration services of the International Chamber of Commerce.	**MERCHANDISE TOTAL** Freight (small package carrier) Import Clearance (by carrier)	US$ 250.00 137.00 50.00
	GRAND TOTAL DDP	**US$ 437.00**

PART IV - AMERICANA

CHAPTER 24 - AN AMERICAN PERSPECTIVE

This chapter will further address many of the points made in the American Viewpoint section of each rule-specific chapter. We can cover them here in a broad-brush manner which is impossible when shown in the context of a single rule.

There are two factors that influence the selection of an Incoterms®[56] rule for a typical American businessperson: the rule itself and how it applies to the way we do business. As mentioned in the start of this book, the 2020 revision is relatively modest in the number of changes from its predecessor. Time will tell just how significant these changes really are. Of at least equal importance are changes in the way business is done in and with the United States.

The following significant rule changes may affect Incoterm® selection.

FCA VERSUS ON BOARD BILL OF LADING

There is an obvious conflict between the requirement of an on-board bill of lading found in many documentary commercial letters of credit and the fact that delivery happens at a place other than on board a vessel in most FCA situations. In an attempt to reconcile these, the FCA rule now provides in B6 that <u>if the parties have agreed</u>, the buyer must <u>instruct</u> the carrier to provide the seller with an on board transport document. The seller must in turn provide the document to the buyer, presumably by means of presentation against a letter of credit. Note the underlines.

This process is not automatic. The parties must have already agreed to this, presumably in the sales contract. The buyer's instructing the carrier is not the same thing as the carrier's agreeing to do so, except as may be provided in the contract of carriage. Further, no carrier will provide an on-board document prior to successful loading. The net result is that while the FCA seller's risk for the condition of the goods has ended, the seller remains at "documentary risk" (i.e. payment risk) through vessel loading; although now mitigated by the buyer's promise to have the document made available.

Aside from vessel loading, specifically obligating the buyer to instruct its carrier to make the transport document available to the seller is a strong reminder not only for FCA but for all F-Group sales contracts. FOB sellers usually need transport documents too. FAS contracts should recite the appropriate document and also provide that it be made available to sellers. This is particularly important for transactions that include document-driven payment terms, such as documentary collections and of course documentary letters of credit.

THE TERRIBLE F-GROUP EXCEPTION

While not a change, this aberration is important to note. Unfortunately, the unwieldy F-Group exception of sellers contracting for main carriage at buyer cost and risk still appears in the 2020 rules. It is unnecessary as the same cost-risk distribution occurs with the C-Group rules. It also avoids a protective feature of CIP and CIF as it has no provision for seller-provided insurance. It disrupts the previous orderly progression from

---

[56] Incoterms® is a trademark of the International Chamber of Commerce, registered in several countries.

EXW to F-Group to C-Group to D-Group. My biggest concern is that it sets the stage for the same widespread confusion found in the UCC, where FOB term is used for both collect and prepaid and in both shipment and arrival contracts. You will find more about the UCC terms in the following chapter.

INSURANCE CHANGE IN THE CIP RULE

Changing the default position from Institute clauses C to A may cause some confusion at first, but in the end conforms to reality for most goods shipped under contracts employing the CIP rule. The insurance default under the CIF rule remains Institute Clauses C. This changes should it serve as wake-up call for all concerned parties to review their insurance procedures. As a start, please re-read the Insurance chapter 8.

FROM DELIVERED AT TERMINAL TO DELIVERED AT PLACE UNLOADED

This is really more semantic than substantial. DAT was originally written around a "terminal" which was loosely defined to be just about any transport-related place. As it was the only rule that tasked the seller with unloading, use quickly spread to include non-transport places such as job sites. Using "terminal" with such locations became quite a stretch, so "terminal" was changed to "place" and the all-important unloading feature was added to the name. To be sure, DPU can and usually will be used with transportation-related places such as piers, container de-consolidators, and of course actual terminals.

The following significant changes in the way we do business may also affect Incoterm selection.

U.S. TARIFF POLICY

Section 232

In 2018, President Trump imposed additional duties of 25% on certain steel items and 10% on certain aluminum items for security reasons under Section 232 of the Trade Expansion Act of 1962. Targeted countries included those with which we have free trade agreements[57] such as Canada and Mexico, as well as the European Union, Japan, India, Turkey and others. Certain trading partners such as Argentina, Australia, Brazil and South Korea were exempted after separate agreements. In addition, certain exemptions became available to some worthy importers who could demonstrate special needs.

Section 301

In 2018, President Trump also imposed significant tariffs on a host of Chinese products for unfair trade practices under Section 301 of the Trade Act of 1974. Additional items and duties have been added and threatened.

New tariff possibilities:

The Commerce Department has concluded a study to determine whether the domestic auto industry is essential for U.S. national security. Results and any threatened tariffs have been postponed until fall 2019.

As of this writing (July 2019) the U.S. Trade Representative is investigating possible new U.S. duties on EU products as a result of a longstanding dispute about government subsidies for large civil aircraft.
Unlike the above, these would come from a likely U.S. win of a dispute at the World Trade Organization and would enjoy more "legitimacy" worldwide.

These tariffs disrupt many U.S. import supply chains. Further, targeted countries promptly filed or are likely to file complaints at the World Trade Organization and many have imposed retaliatory duties on U.S.

[57] As of May 2019, it was determined that Canadian and Mexican steel and aluminum no longer represent a threat to U.S. national security. However, these tariffs can be re-imposed with directed research and the stroke of a pen, in case such imports surge "meaningfully beyond historic volumes of trade over a period of time with consideration of market share."

products. The net effect will be changes in both suppliers and customers. As new trading partners are located, new contract terms will be required. New relationships normally result in a shift towards more conservative payment terms in both directions until mutual confidence can be established. Seller exposure to new markets will involve rethinking transportation and risk transfer. All of the above involve Incoterms® choices.

Increased U.S. tariffs often cause importers to tariff-shop for reclassifications outside the range of targeted items. This can become highly creative, and likely increases Customs' focus on HTSUS classifications.

$800 DE-MINIMIS

All U.S. changes aren't bad. The U.S. Trade Facilitation and Enforcement Act of 2015 increased the de-minimis duty exemption from $200 to a generous $800 of merchandise imported by one person in a single day. This may increase retailer-direct imports which could be detrimental to importing distributors who resell to retailers. (It could also increase consumer-direct imports which are beyond the scope of Incoterms® rules.) As of this writing, the administration is mentioning the possibility of curtailing this to match other countries' de-minimis treatment.

AES

The writer belongs to several trade groups that address members' questions. By far, the most frequently asked questions concern Census' *Foreign Trade Regulations, 15 CFR, Title 15, Part 30.*[58] This, despite continued education efforts on the Bureau's part. The two items drawing the lion's share of questions are Routed Transactions and reportable export value. Detailed coverage is beyond the scope of this book, but we can get you aimed in the right direction.

<u>Parties to the export</u>

These are described with examples in Part 30.3. Census differentiates between "standard export transactions" where the USPPI (seller) directs the export and "routed export transactions" where the FPPI (foreign buyer) authorizes a U.S. agent to facilitate the export of items from the United States and prepare and file EEI.

Under the F-Group rules, the buyer is responsible for main carriage[59] and will often engage a forwarder to do this, creating a routed transaction situation. However, there is an apparent conflict with all three F-Group Incoterms® rules which task the seller with export clearance including export reporting. There are two possible workarounds, either:

amend the contract to make export reporting a buyer obligation

or

have the buyer authorize the USPPI to file the EEI in its behalf.

Either way, the buyer-appointed filer must have written authorization from the buyer to do so.

When a buyer-appointed agent other than the USPPI (i.e. seller) itself files, the following information[60] must be provided to the filer:

- USPPI name, address and EIN or other tax ID number;

---

[58] Thinking up examples for this book gives me renewed empathy for the people who write these regulations. The number of possible international transactions multiplied by the myriad concerned federal agencies must result in many thousands of permutations that must somehow be addressed. Unlike *Lord of the Rings*, there's no one ring to rule them all!

[59] Again, the unfortunate F-Group exception muddies the water.

[60] See Census Foreign Trade Regulations part 30.3e for exact wording

- point of origin for the goods;
- appropriate merchandise code (D or F);
- appropriate Schedule B number, description, quantity and unit of measure, and value of each reportable line item;
- appropriate ECCN export control classification number(s) or enough technical information to determine the ECCN;
- all licensing related information.

My preference when exporting is to file the EEI even with routed transactions. Armed with the buyer's authorization, I instruct the buyer-appointed forwarder to send me the transportation-specific information in writing prior to shipment so I can combine it with my company and product specific information and file promptly. I am therefore sure the filing is correct. Equally important, I get the transportation information, which I then give to my forwarder for competitive freight costs to enable me to steer future sales to the more seller-friendly C-Group rules. Unless there are corrections needed, it takes almost as long to provide the above information to a buyer-appointed forwarder as it does to file. (Incidentally, my company doesn't handle huge numbers of reportable shipments, so this is easy for me to say.) A competing argument can be made, particularly for sellers with many shipments, to leave reporting to the buyer-appointed forwarders. Any necessary corrections take time, and this is more likely to happen when not using your own forwarder. The applicable export control level could also be a factor, but tightly controlled products probably shouldn't be sold on F-Group rules in the first place.

Reportable value

Exporting would be much easier if all reportable shipments were EAR99 and consisted of an invoice for a shipment of a single Schedule B line item, starting with the EXW selling price and separately itemizing pre-carriage (and insurance for pre-carriage). Just ask anyone who has ever manually reported a significant shipment of many different Schedule B items, each valued over $2,500.00, perhaps with different countries of origin, with freight contracted on a door-to door basis. Why the detailed reportable value? That's easy, it matches the entered value regulations for U.S. imports, and enables Census to calculate our balance of trade on an apples-to-apples basis.

Value is described in 30.1 and is defined as follows: *The selling price (or the cost if the goods are not sold) in U.S. dollars, plus inland or domestic freight, insurance, and other charges to the U.S. seaport, airport, or land border port of export.* For goods not sold, the *cost is the sum of expenses incurred in the USPPI's acquisition or production of the goods. (See 30.6(17)).* This presents a problem for filers when the pre-carriage and any insurance costs aren't obvious, as in multimodal transportation. Fortunately, estimates are allowed.[61]

UCC SHIPMENT & DELIVERY TERMS

The going and coming of the UCC terms influences Incoterms® selection so much that we are covering it by itself in the following chapter.

EXPORT LICENSE REQUIREMENTS

Sometimes, export licenses are issued with the condition that the exporter obtain delivery verification to ensure that the goods are actually received by the approved party. Obviously, sellers in these circumstances

[61] For what it may be worth, and again not to be considered legal advice, a former senior Census manager long ago told me off the record that the average value of inland freight had been informally estimated at 3% of the shipment value. Note underlines. The reportable value issue has been around for a long time.

should insist on Incoterms® rules that enable them to contract for carriage (C and D Group). Sellers of goods subject to tight export controls might consider this as a general practice even for shipments where delivery verification is not specifically required. Knowing when, where and to whom the carrier released a shipment of a tightly controlled item can help avoid sleepless nights. Naturally, one must be in a position to give the carrier such instructions, which means contracting with it as in C-Group and D-Group Incoterms® rules.

We will now review some American issues that seem to cause problems for Americans. They certainly keep my phone ringing. They are perennial, and are taken largely from previous versions of this title.

STRETCHING

We should avoid stretching an Incoterms® rule beyond its intended scope. (Again I deliberately ignore the unfortunate F-Group exception where the seller contracts for main carriage at the buyer's cost and risk.) Americans unfamiliar with Incoterms® rules have a tendency to try using an F-Group term accompanied by a final destination in an arrival contract. This comes from the "F.O.B. destination" variations of the former UCC F.O.B. term described in the next chapter. Let's review for emphasis.

Since the FOB Incoterms® rule is used only for waterborne transport, there is only one possible place: on a ship at a port on the seller's side. Same for the FAS Incoterms® rule, except that the only possible place is next to a ship at a port on the seller's side. These two rules are used in shipment contracts. They should never be used with post main carriage places.

The omnimodal FCA rule comes in two flavors, either

a. at the seller's premises (i.e. the place where delivery begins before any carriage)
   or
b. somewhere else on the seller's side after pre-carriage but before any main carriage (often a buyer-appointed carrier's terminal or forwarder's warehouse).

It is used in shipment contracts in alternative a, as the seller delivers at its premises merely by handing the goods over to a carrier. With alternative b., although the seller delivers when the goods arrive at the specified place, that place should always be at the seller's side.

Therefore, the only time it would be appropriate for Americans to use EXW or an F-Group Incoterms® rule with a foreign place would be when the shipment begins there. One example would be sales of goods from a foreign location, as always happens with imports. Another would be local overseas sales of pre-exported U.S. goods from an overseas warehouse. (The overseas warehouse would be the place of shipment, and the costs paid to get them there would presumably have already been folded into the selling price of the goods themselves.)

The converse to stretching is equally true but is nowhere near as widespread. The place with C-Group and D-Group terms should always be somewhere on the buyer's side, as the seller is contracting for carriage to get the goods there.

INCOTERMS® RULES AND OWNERSHIP

This issue comes up again, again and again. The simple answer is that Incoterms® rules do not address title passage. OK, then what does? Answer: either the sales contract or, failing that, local law.

The most logical approach is also the most obvious. Sellers and buyers should agree to when, where and how title passes in their sales contract. Where in the contract? Anywhere except the selected Incoterms® rule. Some possible transfer points include: "upon shipment," "upon arrival," "upon receipt of payment," "upon withdrawal from inventory" (for consignment goods), or just about anywhere else the parties agree. Some countries may have restrictive law on this, but many embrace reasonable freedom of contract.

OK, what happens if it isn't specified? Probably nothing, unless there is a dispute. However, if title passage becomes contentious and the contract is silent, it becomes an issue for the applicable law.
UCC §2-401 appears more or less the same in the contract law of most U.S. states. It provides that for contracts not specifying otherwise, ownership passes when the seller delivers. Incoterms® rules do speak to delivery in A2-B2. Does this mean that the Incoterms® rule determines when ownership passes? No. What the Incoterms® rule states about delivery could trigger title passage by default if the contract is silent and the governing law says so. It's the law, not the Incoterms® rule. What if another law applies? Who knows?

Why not redesign the Incoterms® rules to cover title passage? Several reasons. Laws about ownership differ from country to country. The law that governs much international trade, the United Nations Convention on Contracts for the International Sale of Goods (CISC), doesn't address ownership passage at all. Finally, the most simple reason is that Incoterms® rules speak to shipment and delivery, and one can possess goods without owning them, or own goods without possessing them. (Finance your car?)

REVENUE RECOGNITION

By revenue recognition we mean at what point can a sale be considered an account receivable. This is an important accounting issue, particularly for publicly traded U.S. corporations anxious to satisfy shareholders by exceeding Wall Street analysts' expectations. This means getting financial statements as strong as possible at the close of accounting periods. Revenue recognition regulations have been around for some time, and the Securities and Exchange Commission (www.sec.gov) regulates publicly traded corporations. What have changed are the increased penalties for accounting irregularities imposed by Sarbanes-Oxley (SOX). CEOs and CFOs have become very scrupulous in their insistence that accounting regulations be closely followed.

Revenue recognition rules are not limited to the SEC. The Financial Accounting Standards Board's Generally Accepted Accounting Principles (GAAP) standards for reporting financial information also speak to revenue recognition. Internationally, the International Financial Reporting Standards (IFRS) are becoming the national GAAP for a number of countries.

Delivery as used in Incoterms® rules is a factor in these regulations and standards. Revenue recognition concern can influence the choice of an Incoterms® rule, particularly for publicly traded corporations. D Group Incoterms® rules hold that delivery happens at arrival, usually after all or most of the transportation, therefore delaying revenue recognition. This may put publicly traded U.S. firms at a competitive disadvantage against foreign competition which may not be similarly regulated.
Sometimes, an Incoterms® rule isn't sufficient to satisfy an auditor that delivery took place. I have a firsthand example of a client that had recently become publicly traded and was under strong Wall Street pressure to perform. They manufactured a small product, and frequently received a flurry of orders at month end. They wanted to use the EXW rule and deliver by having the shipments available on their loading dock and notifying their customers, even late at night after their carrier's usual pickup time. Their auditor objected, asking what would happen if the building burned down that night. I do not know the outcome, and mention this merely to illustrate what unintended consequences can attach to Incoterms® rules.

DROP SHIPMENTS

Company A buys product from Company B. Immediately upon receipt, company A ships the product to its customer, company C. Everyone knows who is who and is comfortable with the situation. It quickly occurs to all parties that this practice is inefficient. Shipments from B to A incur freight and time costs in addition to those incurred by shipments from A to C. It would be more efficient for B to sell to A but ship directly to C. This is a typical drop shipment scenario.
Question: what Incoterm® rule should apply?
Answer: unknown.

Reason: there are actually two contracts: one between B as seller and A as buyer, and another between A as seller and C as buyer. Each contract may have its own terms and conditions. It is possible that both contracts use the same Incoterm® rule, but equally possible that each may use a different one. Since drop shipments often take place among related parties, the fact that there are separate agreements is often overlooked.

CHAPTER 25 - WHAT HAPPENED WITH THE UCC SHIPMENT AND DELIVERY TERMS

BACKGROUND

In the United States, the individual states are the primary source of law for commercial transactions. This decentralization fostered the development of commercial laws that differed significantly from state to state. The dramatic development of transportation and communications in the late 1800s greatly expanded interstate commerce, drawing attention to the problems caused by differing state laws.

The National Conference of Commissioners on Uniform State Laws (NCCUSL) was established in 1892 to provide some degree of uniformity in commercial law. In a related development, the American Bar Association established the American Law Institute (ALI) in 1923 to remedy two chief defects in American law: uncertainty and complexity. Together, NCCUSL and ALI began a project to draft an Official Uniform Commercial Code (UCC) in 1940. It was completed over a ten-year period, and all 49 common law states have enacted it[62]. Louisiana, a civil code state, has enacted only those provisions that were compatible with its particular system. Together, ALI and NCCUSL are charged with revising the UCC as needed to address changing business conditions.

WHAT HAPPENED?

The 2010 edition of *Incoterms®*[63] *for Americans*[64]*®* joyfully proclaimed that ALI and NCCUSL had revised the Uniform Commercial Code effective February 2004, and that the shipment and delivery terms found in §2-319 through §2-324 had been deleted. This really did happen. However, fierce opposition by the National Association of Manufacturers and the United States Chamber of Commerce prevailed at the state legislature level. Removal of the shipment and deliver terms was not the problem. Of the 308 pages in the proposed revision, only 4 applied to them. Other issues such as manufacturer liability were far more controversial.

Since contract law is state law in this country, failure to win state approvals doomed the revision. It was quietly rescinded in 2011, so the outmoded shipment and delivery terms remain in the laws of the 49 common law states[65]. As this reversal was done with little fanfare, many readers of this book will be surprised to learn that the old terms are still in the UCC and that they have never left the laws of their states.

Needless to say, this revision / reversal caused considerable confusion. A number of large U.S. companies were happy to learn that the UCC terms had been deleted. They had been using Incoterms® rules for their international business for years, while their domestic trade was conducted under the UCC terms. The use of two different sets of rules caused problems, particularly as some abbreviations appear in both with entirely different meanings. Adopting Incoterms® rules for all purchases and sales made sense, especially when the UCC terms had been slated to disappear on a state by state basis.

Switching became very attractive in 2010 when a new set of Incoterms® rules appeared. Restoration of the old UCC terms makes switching everything to Incoterms® rules less attractive today. However, it does not

---

[62] Adopting the Official UCC, some states opted for alterations. For this reason, the UCC as enacted by one state may differ somewhat from the UCC itself as well as the UCC as enacted by another state. Readers are urged to refer to their particular state's UCC version.

[63] Incoterms® is a registered trademark of the International Chamber of Commerce, registered in several countries.

[64] Incoterms® for Americans® is a registered trademark of International Projects, Inc., and is used by International Projects, Inc. with International Chamber of Commerce permission.

[65] The Civil Code of Louisiana never adopted the UCC shipment and delivery terms. It treats shipment and delivery in Article 23616 and makes specific reference to Incoterms rules as well as the obsolete *Revised American Foreign Trade Definitions of 1941*.

remove the advantage of a common platform of shipment and delivery rules. U.S. companies enjoy considerable freedom of contract. Within reason, buyers and sellers are free to use whatever rules they wish as long as they agree. The catch is to clearly specify what you propose in your contracts. The fact that the old UCC terms remain in law and could apply by default makes it important to recite the rule, accompanying place and version when using Incoterms® rules - particularly in domestic transactions.

So what's the problem with the UCC terms? I admit to some bias here as ever since the 2004 UCC revision I have been advocating use of Incoterms® rules in domestic situations. Check the reasoning and judge for yourself.

- As there are only six UCC terms (plus one document description), they lack the specific nature of the eleven Incoterms® rules.
- The F.O.B. term has evolved to cover almost all possible situations: shipment contracts, destination contracts, freight collect, freight prepaid – to the point where the term itself means nothing without modifiers. Contrast with the FOB Incoterms® rule which can mean one thing only: on a vessel at a port on the seller's side, freight collect.
- They are obsolete, last revised in 1962.
- They are available only in English.
- They are not self-contained.
- They are needlessly complicated.
- They are not well understood, even by Americans. (This may be more the fault of users than the terms themselves.)
- They are far too often used merely as pricing terms.
- They reflect the model for the *Revised American Foreign Trade Definitions*[66] of 1941 (and here my bias really shows.)

Since the old UCC terms remain in state laws, it is now more important than ever to compare them with current Incoterms® rules. To do so, we will paraphrase several pages from the 2010 version of *Incoterms® for Americans* working from the UCC term to the appropriate matchup in Incoterms® 2020 rules. (As mentioned many times in this book, I am not a lawyer, and this is not to be taken as legal advice.) We will be looking at strictly domestic use as no informed party would consider using the UCC terms in international contracts.

UCC §2-319 covers the famous Free on Board (F.O.B.) term, which is by far the most widely used and least understood. Its popularity comes from the fact that it is twisted to fit every conceivable situation, with the result that F.O.B. by itself means nothing. For it to make sense, one must specify both the place and which party is contracting for carriage. Also, the UCC F.O.B. term can be used for either shipment or arrival contracts. By contrast, every Incoterms® 2020 rule clearly indicates this through the delivery point in A2-B2.

Both the UCC F.O.B. and F.A.S. are covered together in §2-319. We will start with the F.O.B. permutations.

UCC §2-319 F.O.B. origin, freight collect: This is probably what users mean by our beloved F.O.B. Factory. The seller is responsible for having the contract goods available at the place where the shipment originates, with no carriage obligation. Delivery occurs at the origin place. However, the seller is not obligated to load the collecting vehicle. The appropriate Incoterms® 2020 rule matchup is Ex Works (EXW), where the seller has no carriage or loading obligations and delivers at the origin place. (It would at first seem that Free Carrier accompanied by the origin place would also match. It doesn't, as under FCA the seller is obligated to load the collecting vehicle.) Like EXW, this UCC term has limited real life application as sellers usually load collecting

[66] The Revised American Foreign Trade Definitions of 1941 were created by the U.S. Chamber of Commerce in 1919 and were last revised in 1941. They were mirrored in the UCC terms to a great extent and presented a rival set of terms to Incoterms®, causing considerable confusion. Although abolished in 1985, they still pop up occasionally when less informed parties attempt to use them.

vehicles. It could work well with small package carriers whose drivers typically load their trucks. Both this UCC term and EXW are designed for use in shipment contracts and for all modes of carriage.

UCC §2-319 F.O.B. origin, car or other vehicle, freight collect: The seller is responsible for having the contract goods available at the place where the shipment originates, with no carriage obligation. Delivery occurs at the origin place. The seller is also obligated to load the collecting vehicle. The appropriate Incoterms® 2020 rule matchup is Free Carrier accompanied by the origin place. Both this UCC term and FCA are designed for use in shipment contracts and for all modes of carriage.

UCC §2-319 F.O.B. origin, freight prepaid: The seller contracts for carriage but delivers by handing the contract goods over to the carrier. This is a good matchup for the CPT or CIP Incoterms® 2020 rules. As mentioned in the Insurance chapter 8, there needs to be some tweaking if CIP is used. Inland Marine insurance claims are typically made by the policy owner, i.e. the seller rather than the buyer. Both this UCC term and CPT and CIP are designed for use in shipment contracts and for all modes of carriage.

UCC §2-319 F.O.B. destination, freight collect: While actually contrary to UCC §2-319b, this unfortunate misuse comes about because the UCC F.O.B. term can be used for both freight collect and freight prepaid carriage and in both shipment and arrival contracts. The seller would have no carriage obligation but would remain responsible for the condition of the contract goods until they arrive. There is no matching Incoterms® 2020 rule, and a moment's thought will reveal why. How can a seller claim for damages on a carrier with which it did not contract? What if the buyer were to us its own truck? Would the seller nevertheless be responsible for the condition of the goods until they arrive?

UCC §2-319 F.O.B. Destination, freight prepaid: The seller is responsible for carriage and delivers when the contract goods arrive. This is an obvious matchup for the Delivered at Place (DAP) Incoterms® 2020 rule. In both cases, the seller contracts for carriage and is responsible for the carrier's performance as delivery does not occur until arrival. If the parties agree that the seller should also be responsible for unloading the goods after they arrive, the new Delivered at Place Unloaded (DPU) rule is available. This UCC term is designed for arrival contracts and all modes of carriage as are all D-Group Incoterms® 2020 rules.

UCC §2-319 F.O.B. vessel: This matches the Incoterms® 2020 FOB rule reasonably well with two exceptions. First, the UCC term makes no provision for string sales while the FOB rule does. Second, the UCC term specifies that unless otherwise agreed, the buyer must make payment against the agreed documents, and that the contract goods themselves are not a substitute for the documents. By contrast, B1 of all Incoterms® 2020 rules simply states that the buyer must pay the price without specifying when, how, or against what. This UCC term and the Incoterms® 2020 rule were designed for shipment contracts and for waterborne carriage.

UCC §2-319 Free alongside (F.A.S.): This matches the Incoterms® 2020 FAS rule reasonably well except that the UCC term makes no provision for string sales while the FAS rule does.

The other UCC terms have their individual UCC part numbers. They are less frequently used, mainly because the F.O.B. term was stretched and twisted around to fit all situations. Also, as will become obvious, Incoterms® rules do a far better job of dividing risk to the contract goods between sellers and buyers.

UCC §2-320 Cost, insurance and freight (C.I.F.) and cost & freight (C.&F.): As with F.O.B. and F.A.S., the UCC covers both terms in the same part. It defines C.I.F. and explains C.& F. as an exception to the insurance requirement. In both cases, the seller contracts for carriage to the agreed port on the buyer's side but delivers by loading the vessel at the port of shipment on the seller's side. These match up reasonably well with the Incoterms® 2020 CFR and CIF rules with two exceptions. First, the UCC terms makes no provision for string sales while the CFR and CIF rules do. Second, the UCC term specifies that unless otherwise agreed, the buyer must make payment against the agreed documents, and that the contract goods themselves are not a substitute for the documents. By contrast, B1 of all Incoterms® 2020 rules simply states that the buyer must pay the price without specifying when, how, or against what. These UCC terms and the CFR and CIF Incoterms® 2020 rules were designed for shipment contracts and for waterborne carriage.

UCC §2-321 Cost, insurance and freight (C.I.F.) and cost & freight (C.&F.) net landed weights: This term takes the C.I.F. and C.&F. terms and adds an additional responsibility to the seller. The seller would weigh the goods prior to shipment, and would be responsible for any difference between the shipped and arrived weights. (Presumably there were mechanisms in place to deal with moisture accumulation common with waterborne shipments.) There are no matchups. Incoterms® 2020 rules look solely at delivery in determining passage of risk for the contract goods from sellers to buyers. As far as how seller-buyer risk is determined, it doesn't matter whether the goods are short one kilo or the ship sinks!

UCC §2-322 Delivery ex ship (D.E.S.): The seller contracts for carriage and remains responsible for the condition of the contract goods until they are unloaded from the vessel at the agreed port on the buyer's side. The new Incoterms® 2020 rule Delivered at Place Unloaded DPU is a good matchup when the agreed place is the quay at the arrival port. Both the UCC term and this rule are used for arrival contracts.

UCC §2-323 Bill of lading: This is not really a shipment and delivery term but a description of a bill of lading document. It's inclusion among shipment and delivery terms illustrates the haphazard way these rules grew. There is no matchup as Incoterms® 2020 rules do not describe documents.

UCC §2-324 No arrival, no sale: This UCC term is used in arrival contracts and provides a way for the buyer to escape the sales contract if the goods fail to arrive or are damaged for reasons beyond the seller's control. It also refers to UCC §2-613 Casualty to identified goods. Besides terminating the contract for non-arrival, this allows the buyer to accept goods at reduced pricing in cases of partial loss or damage. Incoterms® rules do not operate this way. Instead, they focus on delivery for risk transfer.

INDEX

A

Acceptance (contracts) 17
Adventure (insurance) 33
AES 141
Airport to airport 30
Airport to door 30
All risk 6, 3.43, 97
Allocation of costs (A9-B9) 5,6
American Institute of Marine Underwriters (AIMU) 33
Arrival contracts 12
Average (insurance) 33

B

Bilateral contracts 17

C

C-Group rules 87
Carriage (A4-B4) 5, 28
Carriage and Insurance Paid (CIP) 97
Carriage Paid To (CPT) 89
Checking/Packaging/Marking (A8-B8) 5
Contracts: (arrival 12, carriage 28, 30, customs brokerage 28, forwarding 28, insurance 28, payment 28, shipment 12)
Cost and Freight (CFR) 103
Cost Insurance and Freight (CIF) 109

D

D-Group rules 115
Delivered At Place (DAP) 117
Delivered at Place Unloaded (DPU) 123, 140
Delivered At Terminal (DAT) 123, 140
Delivered Duty Paid (DDP) 131
Delivery (A2-B2) 5
Delivery / Transport Document (A6-B6) 30
(EXW 42, FCA 56,59, FAS 74, FOB 83, CPT 90, CIP 99, CFR 104, CIF 110, DAP 118, DPU 124, DDP 132)
De-minimis 133, 141
Door to door 30
Door to port (airport) 30
Drop shipments 9, 14, 144
Duty drawback 4

E

Entity list (EAR §744) . . . 3
Explanatory notes . . . 5
Export / import control document (EXW 42, FCA 56, 59, FAS 75, FOB 83, CPT 91, CIP 99, CFR 104, CIF 110, DAP 118, DPU 124, DDP 132)
Export Control Reform . . . 3
Export / Import clearance (A7-B7) . . . 5
(See Export / import control document)
EX Works (EXW) . . . 41

F

F-Group exception . . . 15, 51, 139
F-Group rules . . . 51
Foreign Trade Regulations (FTR) . . . 15, 141
Free Alongside (UCC term) . . . 149
Free Alongside Ship (FAS) . . . 73
Free Carrier (FCA) . . . 53
Free In and Out (FIO) . . . 31
Free In Liner Out . . . 31
Free of (insurance) . . . 33
Free of Particular Average (FPA) . . . 6, 34, 110
Free On Board (FOB) . . . 81
Free On Board (UCC term) . . . 148

G

GAAP . . . 9, 144
General average . . . 34, 111
General Obligations (A1-B1) . . . 5
Global Magnitsky sanctions . . . 3
Group chart . . . iv

I

IFARS . . . 9, 144
Import clearance (DDP) . . . 131
(See also Export / import control document)
Incoterms® 2020 official ICC book . . . iii
Institute Cargo Clauses (LMA/IUA) . . . 6, 33, 97, 110
Insurance (A5-B5) . . . 5, 33
Insurance topics: (carrier – forwarder provided 35, inland marine 35, marine cargo 33)

J

JCPOA (Iran nuclear) . . . 4

L

Liner terms 30
Liner In Free Out (LIFO) 31
Loading
(EXW 41, FCA 55 & 58, FAS 74, FOB 82, CPT 90, CIP 98, CFR 104, CIF 110, DAP 117, DPU 123, DDP 131)
Low sulfur regulation (UN IMO) 4
Low value import 3, 133, 141

M

Main carriage 29
(CPT 90, CIP 98, CFR 104, CIF 110, DAP 117, DPU 123,DDP 131)

N

Non-liner terms 30
Notices (A10-B10) 5

O

Offers (contract) 17
Omnimodal iv
On board 6, 54, 59, 139
On-carriage 29
(CPT 90, CIP 98, DAP 117, DPU 123, DDP 131)
Ownership 143

P

Parties to the export (AES) 141
Payment considerations
(EXW 42, FCA 56, 59, FAS 75, FOB 83, CPT 91, CIP 99,CFR 104, CIF 110, DAP 118, DPU 124, DDP 132)
Place (start, departure, arrival, end) 25
Port (airport) to door 30
Port to port 30
Pre-carriage 29
(EXW 42, FCA 55, 59, FAS 74, FOB 82, CPT 90, CIP 98, CFR 104, CIF 110, DAP 117, DPU 123, DDP 131)
Proforma invoices 17

R

Reportable value (AES) 15, 142
Revenue recognition 144
Routed Transactions 141
(FCA 61, FAS 76, FOB 84)

S

Sales contract considerations 13
Shipment contracts 12
Stretching (Incoterms® rule uses) 14, 143
String sales
(FAS 74, FOB 81, CPT 90, CIP 98, CFR 103, CIF 109)
Sue and labor 34

T

Tariff policy (U.S.) 140
Task lines 5
Terms of shipment & delivery 12
Trans Pacific Partnership 4
Transfer of Risks (A3-B3) 5
Transportation legs 29

U

Uniform Commercial Code shipment & delivery terms 147
United States Council for International Business (USCIB) iii
Unloading
(FCA 59, FAS 74, FOB 82, CPT 90, CIP 98, CFR 104, CIF 110, DAP 117, DPU 123, DDP 131)

V

Variants (to Incoterms® rules) 15
Verified Gross Mass (VGM) 3